Memories of

Lancaster

Memories of

Lancaster

Sharon Lambert

TEMPUS

Frontispiece:

Above: A Hope Street party celebrating the Coronation of George VI in 1937.

Below: The Hope Street VE Day party, 1945.

First published 2005

Tempus Publishing Limited
The Mill, Brimscombe Port,
Stroud, Gloucestershire, GL5 2QG

British Library Cataloguing in Publication Data.
A catalogue record for this book is available from the British Library.

ISBN 0 7524 3719 4

Typesetting and origination by Tempus Publishing Limited
Printed in Great Britain

Contents

About the Author

Sharon Lambert (*née* Deehan) was born in Lancaster and has lived in the city all her life. She studied history as a mature student and graduated from Lancaster University with a BA and a PhD. Her doctoral thesis was based on an oral history of Irish women's emigration. She has taught social history courses at all levels, for Lancaster University, the University of Central Lancashire, the Workers Educational Association and the Adult College, Lancaster. She is an honorary research fellow at Lancaster University's Centre for North West Regional Studies and now works as a freelance social historian and oral history and reminiscence consultant, but continues to teach adults in the community. She writes a monthly 'Life-History' column in the *Lancaster Guardian* and her previous publications include: *Monks Martyrs and Mayors: The History of Lancaster's Roman Catholic Community and Cathedral* (1991); *Irish Women in Lancashire, 1922-1960: Their Story* (2001); *Fumigating the Cat and other stories from the Marsh History Group* (edited with Nigel Ingham, 2004). In 2003 she received a British Association of Local History Publication Award for an article about her community history classes on the Marsh Estate, Lancaster.

Acknowledgements

My thanks go to Lancaster City Museums for permitting the use of some photographs from their collection. I am extremely grateful to Joan Bradshaw and members of the Lancaster Family History Society for their generosity in allowing me to reproduce images of 1960 street scenes from one of their calendars, especially at such short notice and without cost. I owe the biggest debt of all to the people whose memories are recorded here, and who also provided most of the images. Over the past decade I have interviewed many fascinating people for a variety of oral history projects and collected hundreds of taped recordings and transcripts. Nevertheless, I still approach each new interview with the anticipation that I will learn something new, and I haven't been disappointed yet. Every respondent, even the fiftieth person I have asked the same question of, possesses the unique quality of relating a memory from their own perspective. Some of the recollections in this book were collected from interviews conducted for past projects, some were recorded during reminiscence or local history classes and some were gathered specifically for this publication. My sincere thanks go to the following people for so generously sharing their memories and photographs and recording a part of our city's history from their unique perspective for future generations to enjoy:

Charlie Adams, Val Atkinson, Roberta Bateson, Gwen Bell, Jim Bell, Jean Brotheridge, Betty Cummings, Patsy Cuffe, Maureen Deehan, Jimmy Downham, Gloria Dunstan, Audrey Entwistle, Joan Herman, Lillian Hennedy, Mary Hodgson, Gina Holden, Bob Howson, Jack Hurtley, Joan Kimpton, Ken Lambert, Fred Lewis, Herbert Lowe, Bridie McLaughlin, Maureen Palwankar, Vasant Palwankar, Peggy Phillips, Robin Preston, Hanna Przewozniak, John Pye, Ken Riley, Marlene Russell, Freda Simpson, Jean Slatter, Marlene Snape, Bill Stockdale, John H. Taylor, Eileen Varey, Joan Varey, Jack Watson, Ralph Wilson, Margaret Yates.

Introduction

Everywhere and everybody has a history. Yet, for too long, the study of history was concentrated on the extraordinary events, places and characters of the past. With the development of social history, however, came recognition that everyday details of ordinary people's lives make a valuable contribution to our understanding of history. Social history is about the ordinary as much as the extraordinary and, to my mind, oral history is the best method of recording the details of people's lives from their own perspective. I was first attracted to oral history for its potential to democratise the study of history when used as a means of 'writing history from below' and this attraction has only increased with experience. In every society (at least to this writer's knowledge) the ordinary people have vastly outnumbered the privileged or outstanding ones, so it makes perfect sense to regard history from that more representative vantage point. This history of Lancaster is unashamedly written from the perspective of ordinary Lancastrians. And who better to inform us of what life was really like in this city in the past century?

'Around Town' is a curious title for the first chapter of a book about the *city* of Lancaster but like many Lancastrians I tend to frequently switch between town and city when describing my home place. How many Lancaster City Football fans, for example, say they are going to watch 'the Town' play? It could be attributed to the fact that Lancaster has been a city for less than seventy years but I suspect that it has more to do with the scale of the place when compared to other cities which are usually much larger and impersonal than ours. Since 1937 Lancaster has officially been a city (and we appreciate that honour) but it thankfully still retains the scale, charm and friendliness of its market town origins, along with a pride in its historic county town status of course. We have the best of both worlds really and that is my excuse for my ambiguity!

Many of the memories are from 'born and bred' Lancastrians who can remember when Lancaster was actually still a town. There are vivid recollections of streets that have long since been demolished. Few people visiting the wasteland that is Edward Street Car Park today would recognise it as the site of Marlene Snape's childhood memories: where a bustling community was regularly disturbed by the forays of herds of cattle making their way to the auction house through narrow streets of terraced houses. Likewise, the Pointer Roundabout, now so busy with twenty-first-century traffic, covers the demolished Boundary Street home and childhood playground of the young Jimmy Downham, where in the 1920s he and his mates played football with a pig's bladder from the slaughterhouse. Youngsters today could scarcely risk dashing across China Street to chase their pals round Covell Cross as Jack Watson did from his home in the Black Bull. Not only have streets changed dramatically but lifestyles have too. Jean Slatter's recollections of working in Lancaster's biggest pawn shop on Rosemary Lane show how a lot of working-class people, particularly housewives, managed a weekly budget in a way far removed from today's credit card transactions.

Working-class Lancastrians experienced dramatic changes in their housing conditions between the two world wars. As a result of successive government acts, municipal housing and slum clearance programmes were carried out and Lancaster's first council housing was built at Bowerham in the 1920s. This was followed by more estates including Ryelands, the Marsh, Beaumont and Newton. Alongside this, many town-centre dwellings were demolished. Visitors to the City Museum in Market Square can see photographs of many of the courts, yards and streets that were cleared during this period in their collection of contemporary photographs taken by Sam Thompson. The chapter on homes and neighbourhoods provides memories of this transition from town-centre housing to the new council estates. Interestingly, they show how not just individual families but small settled communities of whole streets and courts were often simply transplanted to a new place. The people that sisters Betty and Joan Hargreaves recalled living alongside in Blue Anchor and Chancery Lanes in the town centre were their neighbours again when they moved onto the new Marsh Estate in 1935.

The chapter on leisure highlights the enormous popularity of the cinema in the 1930s and 1940s when people remembered Lancaster as having no fewer than seven picture houses, all showing different films and often with very long queues. Dancing was another popular pastime, not the solitary 'dancing round your handbag disco style' of this envious writer's generation but ballroom dancing to big bands and later jiving to rock 'n' roll music. Neighbouring Morecambe, then in its heyday as a seaside resort, provided ample ballrooms for dancers and the Alexandra Hotel appears to have been Lancaster's most popular dance hall. A more gentle age is recalled by Bill Stockdale's lovely memory of 'The Walk', where lads and lasses met and chatted as they followed an orchestrated route round the town centre every Sunday evening.

The chapter on working lives reminds us how much employment in the city has changed over the past century. Factories such as Williamson's, Storey's and Lansil, institutions like the Moor and Royal Albert Hospitals and the famous Waring & Gillow's cabinet makers were household names here at one time but have long ceased to be our major employers of labour. There is also an example of an occupation that will never be seen again – the knocker-up.

Multi-culturalism might be a relatively new term in our vocabulary but it is not a new concept in Lancaster. A personal memory of attending Cathedral School in the 1960s is of many pupils being the children of Irish (as in my case), Polish or Italian immigrants and in the book Charlie Adams recalls that, due to his Irish ancestry, he was affectionately known as 'Paddy' Adams in the same school four decades earlier. The chapter 'Moving Here' highlights some fascinating, and indeed sometimes heroic personal experiences from some of our citizens who came here from other countries.

The section on sport includes characteristically modest memories from one of Lancaster's best-loved citizens, the inimitable Jimmy Downham, who over many years has passed on the skills of his beloved game to at least hundreds, and very probably thousands of youngsters.

History comes to life when we can connect with people in the past. Read on and enjoy these memories of Lancaster and hopefully, like me, you will be charmed by the honesty, humility and good humour of the narrators. They have taken many social changes in their stride and contributed much to the Lancaster we enjoy today. We walk in their shadows.

one

Around Town

Carthorses were everywhere

We used to go from Dallas Road School to Cable Street Baths. We'd go over by the castle and down by the Judges' lodgings, down Bridge Lane and have a chatter to old Sailor Bill. I don't know what his real name was. He was just a character that everybody knew. I don't think anybody knew his proper name actually. He used to sit on the flags in front of his house on Bridge Lane and draw your portrait on the flagstones and if we had any money on us we used to throw it into his hat. And then we went along Cable Street, stopped at the blacksmith's on the corner to see him shoeing the horses before we went to the baths. The blacksmith's was just short of the corner of Water Street and Cable Street. It was a big opening and it just opened into like a stable and there was the furnace there and the horses used to be tied up. We used to stand and watch the blacksmith for hours with these red hot horseshoes. He was a great old bloke, I

forget his name. There were horses all around. Next to the blacksmiths is a passageway (it's still there) that goes down into like a yard and through there Brooke Bond's Tea used to have these little Trojan vans. They were like a little three-wheeler van and they used to make a funny noise, they didn't sound like an engine. You could hear them as soon as they came out, coming down the road. They delivered to all the shops.

We used to watch water polo on a Friday night at Cable Street Baths before they went to the new baths (Kingsway) and we all stopped going to watch it then. W. & J. Pye's had a big warehouse just past the baths where they used to keep all their garden manures, potash and all that. The bloke who looked after that for them, old Bert Sandham with a long beard, was the resident Father Christmas for the Infirmary. He did Father Christmas every year up at the Infirmary. He was a right jovial character.

Lower Thurnham Street, with Winskill's toffee shop on the corner, and the town hall in 1960.

Carthorses were everywhere on the roads then. From West Road, we went over the railway bridge to go up to the castle and there was a place on the right there with windows down near the ground because the stables were more-or-less under the road. All the carthorses for the railway were kept there. They used to go in a morning, get these carthorses, bring them round past Castle Station, across the road and down the side of Sibsey Street into the goods yard there. Then they used to connect them up to a cart, turn right over the bridge and into town and then they'd start delivering with these horse and carts.

Bill Stockdale (b. 1923)

Right: Bridge Lane in the 1920s.

Below: W. & J. Pye's warehouse in Fleet Square, facing on to Cable Street, in 1905.

Murphy's and the Home and Colonial

I remember Murphy's in the market, that was a grand place. You could get pots, pans, dustbins, pegs, and they always used to sell this brown soap. It was like disinfectant soap that you scrubbed your oilcloth with and it brought floors up beautiful. I never saw it after Murphy's. Because you didn't have fitted carpets then; just coconut matting that if you knelt on it you got a pattern on your knees. And then when you picked it up it was full of dust underneath, horrible. There's a big picture of Murphy's up in the market now. They'd everything for cleaning, anything you wanted you could get there. And there was the Home and Colonial on Penny Street that sold bacon, cooked meats, tea, sugar, butter, everything. You could get all your week's rations there.

Maureen Deehan, *née* Riley (b. 1935)

Cuthbert's Chemist

There was Cuthbert's Chemist on the corner of Cable Street and North Road, that was a big chemist's. It went right round the corner of both streets. It was across the road from where Sainsbury's is, on the corner, it's a car park now. There was a block of houses next to it on Cable Street, where the fire station is now. My mam's sister, Auntie Alice, lived on there till they knocked them all down and moved her on to Mainway. Then there was Macari's next door to it: they had a café on North Road that we used to go in for a cup of tea and a bite to eat. Woodhouse's fish shop was next door to Macari's on North Road for years before they moved to Church Street. I used to go in there from work. I worked at the slipper factory on Leonardgate and we used to go through the ginnel, where Territorial Army was, to it. I remember there was a toffee shop

Common Garden Street with the market entrance to the right of the Black Horse Hotel, 1960

Cuthbert's Chemist at the corner of Cable Street and North Road, 1960. This junction was popularly known as Cuthbert's Corner. Macari's Café sign on North Road is just visible on the extreme left. The site is now a car park.

on Market Street, Lyon's Toffee Shop. It used to be on that side where the Blue Anchor pub is now. And T.D. Smith's had grocer's shops all over. There was one on Penny Street, one in Dalton Square, a big one on the corner of Market Street near Stan Gray's barbers: it's the card shop now. And there was one across from Stott's fish shop on West Road.

Lillian Hennedy (b. 1934)

Butcher's shops
There used to be a lot of butcher's shops in town: Slinger's and Taylor's butchers going up to the market off Penny Street, and Kinloch's Pork Butcher's sold bacon, sausages and pies.

Their pies were nice. They sold tripe as well. You don't hear of it now but a lot of people used to eat tripe, and pig's trotters and pig's head. Woodhouse's fish shop used to sell lovely tripe and onions when it was on North Road. And you used to be able to get a wrap-up at the butcher's. You'd maybe get a little bit of everything in it: steak, chops, liver, sausage. We'd say now a mixed grill type of thing but you used to call it a wrap-up.

Patsy Cuffe (b. 1940)

The pawn shop
I used to work in the pawn shop on Rosemary Lane. I started there about 1949, I think. He

A 1948 advertisement.

took me on originally to help with the book-keeping, or to teach me book-keeping, but thrown in with that was keeping the shop clean, dusting the parcels. You can't imagine that because there were piles and piles and piles of parcels. The first morning I started there, the man in charge was a Mr Phillips who was the manager. It was a Carnforth company, George Thompson I think it was. There were two branches; there was one on Brock Street and the one on Rosemary Lane.

The one on Brock Street was where they kept most of the jewellery and the clocks and stuff like that. On Rosemary Lane it was mainly clothing, bedding, although he did take jewellery in there. Anything really that was in good condition he would take. But the first morning I started there he gave me a tin of Brasso and two dusters and said: 'Right, you have to clean all this brassware every morning.' There was handles on the doors, a great brass rail along the pledge office, lock covers and all kind of things. But there was also the three brass balls outside! And I was nearly in tears. I took me time and I thought I'll have to leave that till last 'cause I don't know how to do that. And I'm standing there with me polish in me hand after I'd done everything else and he said: 'What's wrong love?' And I said, 'I don't know how I'm gonna do them, I don't think I can reach!' They were way up, you know. And he said, 'Oh, you don't clean them.' I said 'Oh, well that's alright then.'

But it was interesting in that … I mean, you don't realise when you're young, I mean my mother used the pawn shop for years. And it was a case of keeping a bundle of stuff that was in good condition, you know: bedding, tablecloths, and that was kept specially for the pawn shop. So if she run short of money, which she frequently did on a Monday morning, it was down to the pop shop, get five shillings, or whatever it was, to last her until pay day. I'm not quite sure what the interest was. I know it wasn't a lot, it was something like a ha'penny a week I think, on top of what you … so if you were getting say five shillings on a bundle, you were paying five and a penny maybe back. I don't know quite what that was. But I know that if you didn't redeem it within a certain time, you lost it. And they used to have a sale, every three months or so, where all the stuff that people had lost on pledges they sold off in the shop. It was quite a big shop. In fact, the shop front is still there on Rosemary Lane, it's now a restaurant called 'Ask', the one where all the cars keep going through. Well that was the shop front but there was a passageway from Lower Church Street, which is still there, went right through to Rosemary Lane and on there was the pledge office. And there's still a couple of little shops down there that used to be part of the pawn shop. One used to be McCormack's book shop and I think there's another little one called Rosemary and Thyme. The pledge office was where part of the pub is now on Lower Church Street. I think it was down the alleyway so that people wouldn't see you. I mean, although you can say now there was no shame in it, but people didn't like you to know they were going to the pawn shop. Or were going to the 'Pop Shop' or 'Uncle's,' as they used to call him, Mr Phillips.

But I once went up to Brock Street, they sent me up to Brock Street to clean up there, and they give me a bucket of wet sand, would you believe, and sent me upstairs. And I think it hadn't been dusted for about twenty five years. He said 'Sweep the floor and then when you've done that, dust the parcels off.' And this bucket of sand, I had to throw the wet sand out 'cause there was that much dust. It was unbelievable. I was filthy when I'd finished. That was my brief couple of days up at Brock Street and then I went back down to Rosemary Lane. It was wonderful, I loved it down there. And people used to come in and you knew if they weren't going to redeem, because sometimes they didn't, they would get as much money as they possibly could on their bundle and then take off. But then people used to sell their tickets as well, if you couldn't afford to get it out you would sell it on to somebody and they would go and get your bundle… Oh the suits on a Monday! Well the wives used to come on a Monday with their husbands suits, right, into the pawn shop and on Friday night take 'em out. Many a time the fellers didn't know anything about this. And I know Mr Phillips used to stay behind on a Friday night in case anybody couldn't make it before the shop shut. And he would wait there because sometimes, if they missed, they'd come into the shop on a Saturday morning with a shiner, you know, they'd walked into the cupboard door! But it was quite a hefty trade was that. It was a lifeline for a lot of people, the pawn shop. I know my mother couldn't have managed without it…

I think one of the funniest things that happened to me when I worked there was: this man came in with a watch or something, I can't quite remember what it was, and I used to have to write the tickets out. So I had to ask him for his name, and I had to ask him for his address. And he said 'One Anderton Ten Stonewell.' And I thought that's a weird address! And I said to him 'Pardon?' and he said 'One Anderton Ten Stonewell!' Well it didn't make sense but I wrote it on the ticket anyway. And then I realised, a long time afterwards, he was a cockney. And it was One hundred and ten! His address was 110 Stonewell.

Jean Slatter, *née* Clarkson (b. 1934)

She pawned his suit in secret

Me mam was hard up one day, God rest her soul, she needed money for something, and she put me dad's suit in the pawn shop on Monday, but she'd to make sure it come out for him going out for a pint on Friday. She got his wages from Dilworth's and she sent me sister Lil straight to pawnshop on Rosemary Lane with the little ticket to get the suit out for him coming home at night. He never knew, he'd have hit the roof if he had. Oh no, you kept that secret.

Maureen Deehan, *née* Riley (b. 1935)

Ma Watts's penny chunks

I went to the 'Nashy School' – the Boys National School, in St Leonardgate. Across from the school there used to be a little shop, Watts's, and the lady in it was always known to us schoolkids as Ma Watts. She used to sell milk, bread, toffees and everything but the speciality for us kids was going into the shop and getting what they called 'a penny chunk.' Ma Watts used to get a small unsliced loaf, cut it into four chunks and put these chunks in oven to toast. She used to put a bit of butter on them and they were lovely and hot. We used to nip out o' school at playtime just to get these penny chunks. And we used to get them after coming out of Kingsway Baths. You were starving after coming out from swimming and they were lovely. She used to sell more penny chunks than 'owt else in that shop.

Ken Lambert (b. 1929)

St Leonardsgate in 1927, with the Grand Theatre on the right.

We were known for a bleach called Lanry

Our family had a wholesale and retail grocers in Moor Lane for over a hundred years. B.R. & W.H. Riley. I worked there for twenty years and me father retired in 1963. His brother (B.R.) had died so he ran it. We were known for a bleach called Lanry, that's how we got going. We were retailers, my father was a confectioner and we had a retail confectioner's and grocer's. But the person who invented Lanry, one of them, lived in Morecambe and he came round and asked if my father and uncle would stock it. And they said we'll try it and he said 'we'll let you have it to yourself.' A few months later he arrives again saying everybody was asking for Lanry and he'd given them sole agency and he wanted to expand it. We were only the one shop, selling a few dozen a week if we were lucky. So my father said they would buy a little van and take it round to the shops for him. And through going round to the shops with this Lanry they started asking for other things. This was before the war when there were no supermarkets. So they started selling everything and we kept the retail shop but finished up mainly as wholesalers selling to shops. Up to finishing in 1963 we were selling five hundred dozen bottles of Lanry a week to shops. We started selling Lanry just before the war and it got us going in the wholesale business. We were just retail confectioners before that. My father told me he used to sell pies to the girls going to the mill above before six o'clock in the morning and he was still selling to people after the second house pictures at night. We built our wholesale business on Lanry.

My father retired in 1963 and after a long discussion I decided not to take over, thank goodness, because it was getting very competitive. So I was invited by Derek Braithwaite, funnily enough at the same time, to see if I was interested in starting a sports shop. Then Derek Braithwaite and I set up a sports shop in Stonewell before Lancaster was all reorganised.

Looking down St Nicholas Street from Horseshoe Corner, 1960.

T.D. Smith's general grocery shop in Dalton Square, 1960

Cable Street in 1960. The bus is passing the former Cable Street Baths. Sainsbury's now stands on the site, its entrance corresponding with that of Hargreaves' wholesale fruit and vegetable warehouse in the picture.

St Leonardgate in 1960, looking down to the Grand Theatre.

That was in 1963. We started in a condemned shop in Stonewell, it used to be a shoe shop, opposite the post office in Stonewell. There was still Church Street and Nicholas Street those days. We were there for about three years and then we moved to Market Square. I was in Market Square and we had a shop in Marketgate and we had a shop at the university and we had a shop at Euston Road, Morecambe. Derek finally left and he went to work for the Earl of Spencer, Lady Di's people, and his wife went as well. And then I finally moved to Church Street for the last six years and I finished on Church Street. We had a successful business and good staff.

Ken Riley (b. 1928)

Watching the police on Lucy Street

I was born in Lucy Street in January 1917, one of ten children: five boys and five girls. Me mother used to tell me that I was six months old when White Lund blew up in 1917 but she always added 'but you weren't to blame!' That was a comforting thought for me. Lucy Street was under the shadow of the town hall clock. It's a car park now. Living on Lucy Street everything seemed handy to me: my school, St Peter's, was 200 yards away, the police station was just across the road, the fire brigade was just across the road and the shops were just a couple of hundred yards away. And of course we got to know all the policemen and firemen and all the town hall people with living nearby. Whenever there was a fire all the people used to come to the end of the streets and watch the old Merryweather fire engine come out of the fire station on George Street and apart from the firemen there always used to be one or two policemen on it as well.

In the twenties and thirties it wasn't the county police it was the Lancaster Borough Police and the funny thing about that is that they had their own Black and White Minstrel group and they used to perform at various functions in town, the police's Black and White Minstrel group. In fact, every Christmas when I was young the borough police used to

Lancaster Fire Brigade's new Merryweather engine in 1912.

and they used to switch their hand lamps on and as they walked through town they'd try every shop door handle just to make sure that everything was secure.

You always seemed to know when Lord Ashton was going to come through the town. A line of policemen used to come out in front of the town hall with the sergeant and one used to be posted to Skerton Bridge, another to Stonewell, another to Dalton Square, another to Penny Street Bridge and another up to Ashton Road. Because he used to travel from his house in Ryelands Park to Ashton Hall. But as he came through the town the blinds were drawn in his posh car because at that time he seemed to have transferred all his affection to St Anne's-on-Sea and he seemed to have fallen out with Lancaster for some reason, I think it was something political. The children all about, they knew there was something coming off. They'd see so much police activity and fire brigade activity, they seemed to know and sense what was coming off. So we all went out to watch. Oh yes. But he always had the blinds drawn so that you couldn't see him. Lord Ashton died in 1930 and he was the main employer in town.

Charlie Adams (b. 1917)

have a children's party for their own children and they used to invite the kids from round the immediate area as well. It was something we really looked forward to, I went twice, and we had a jolly good feed there, jelly and cus-tard etcetera, and we always come away with a 'Lucky Bag' and a toy or else a nice, coloured, woolly winter scarf, something like that. The party was in the basement of the town hall, what we called the Parade Room. The police-men I remember from that time were Chief Constable Vann, PC Cowley, PC Connors, PC Blackburn and PC Nobby Clark. Another thing that I used to notice was that on a dark winter's night the policemen would walk out into the front of the town hall and the sergeant would direct them to different areas,

Guns at the castle

I spent some hours up around the castle as a boy. They used to have guns up there. We used to go up West Road and turn into the castle at the top of Long Marsh Lane. There was some grass on the left-hand side and then there was a big place, paved off with chains round, where there were Howitzers and different types of guns. There were about eight guns in there that they'd used in the First World War. When the war started they just cleared the lot out, anything that was metal had to go to be melted down like.

Bill Stockdale (b. 1923)

Lancaster City Fire Brigade outside their station behind the town hall in 1937. Joe Parkinson is on the left of the back row. Until 1941 the Chief of Police was also the Chief Fire Officer and Chief Constable Vann is in the centre of the front row with the Deputy Fire Chief, Inspector Walker of the Police Force, on the front row third from the right.

The display of guns outside Lancaster Castle in 1940, probably not long before they were taken to be melted down for the war effort.

I remember seeing the big guns outside the castle. Some were from the Crimean War and some from World War One. They'd all been captured by the King's Own Regiment in those two wars.

John Pye (b. 1925)

Isolation Hospital

In the early days, in the 1920s, I remember the old isolation hospital down on the Marsh: and that was situated where the builder's yard is at the other side of Williamson's factory, right on the side of the Lune, that was the isolation hospital then. Anybody with scarlet fever and infectious diseases, that used to be down there, they used to take them down there in a horse-drawn van. The reason why that finished there was because it used to flood. And there was one particular high flood in the 1920s, when so many cattle and sheep were drowned there because the water came up about three feet deep over those fields. And a gentleman by the name of Bill Jackson, who was the licensee of the Blue Anchor Hotel, went to help. And I mean the Blue Anchor Hotel that was on the quay at that time, near the stone bridge there was the Blue Anchor Hotel in those days. There were three pubs along the quay at that time. That's why the middle one, people used to refer to it as 'the middle house'. There was the Blue Anchor at one side, the Wagon and Horses at the other, and the George and Dragon, that was the middle house… Of course with the isolation hospital being down there, and so much flooding going on, they built a new isolation hospital over on Beaumont. That was in 1934.

Charlie Adams (b. 1917)

Damside Street before a bus station was built on the site in the 1930s.

The Cathedral

I was born in 1925 on Grasmere Terrace. My dad, Richard, worked at Storey's for fifty-two years, he was a lorry driver, and my mother's name was Dorothy. I had one brother and three sisters. Then when I was about four we moved on Prospect Street, next to Papes's shop. A lot of our relations already lived on Prospect Street: my grandma, two aunties, an uncle, lived at various houses along there. In 1930, when I was five, I went to the Cathedral, the best school in Lancaster. I started school with Margaret Horn from Number 20 and many years later she pulled my leg saying I cried on my first day. Mr Sowerby was the headmaster and we called him 'Pop' Sowerby.

I've been going to Mass in the cathedral from the day I could walk and I started being an altar server when I was about eight, with Tommy Dakin. When we used to go school on a Monday, the teacher had a register and asked who went to Mass on Sunday. There was myself and Tommy, who became Canon Dakin: 'Mass and Benediction twice Miss, Holy Communion once.' 'Cause you were only allowed to go to Communion once. She said 'What do you mean?' I said, 'Well we're both altar servers Miss.' I remember being called out of class by the priest and going in a taxi to the Moor Hospital to serve Mass. It was very scary as every door we went through was locked after us but after Mass we had a scrumptious breakfast before going back to school.

Of course it was all Latin when I went to Mass as a boy. It was drummed into us was Latin actually, especially with Pop Sowerby. I enjoy the solemn Latin Mass but I'm with-it now, I move with the times. In the old days, you had a priest right up on the altar with his back to the congregation, little altar boys knelt with him, chuntering away in Latin and the people weren't taking part. Now,

St. Peter's church interior, c.1910. It became a cathedral when the Catholic diocese of Lancaster was established in 1924.

everybody's taking part. Although I liked the Latin Mass, I think I'd rather have it as it is today. I've known all five of the Catholic bishops in my time. I met the first bishop, Bishop Pearson, and I served Bishop Flynn, then Bishop Foley, Bishop Brewer was a big friend of mine, and then of course we've got Bishop Pat [O'Donoghue], who I have a bit of banter with.

I remember Dr Dixon, Reggie Dixon, who was the organist at the cathedral for many, many years. He lived on Cannon Hill and he always had high heels on his shoes and earrings in. When Dr Dixon played the organ he nearly blew the roof off. I remember one time: they had to do some work above the high altar. It was a Quaker who was doing the job and when he'd completed the job, he said to our head bell-ringer, Mr Rainford, 'Could you get a team of bell ringers to ring

A Corpus Christi procession passing in front of the cathedral, *c.1950*

A Corpus Christi procession in 1952

Cathedral bell ringers in 1947. John Pye is second from the left on the front row.

the bells for about a quarter of an hour?' He said, 'I'm gonna put a glass of water on one of these new beams.' After about a quarter of an hour, when we came down, there was not a drop spilt. So then he got Dr Dixon to play the organ as he always played it and there was water all over the place. There was more vibration off the organ than the bells.

Years ago we used to have Corpus Christi processions round the cathedral. Every section of the parish took part, there used to be hundreds there, it was a real long procession. All the boys and girls used to get dressed up, the Guides and Scouts, the Children of Mary, the Catholic Mothers, the Men's Sodality, the Sea Scouts, everybody used to take part. The Blessed Sacrament was carried. We used to come out of church, up the churchyard, down East Road, along St Peter's Road, up Balmoral Road, through the house gate and back in across the lawn. And as the first part of the procession was getting near the church, the back part was just coming out. In May, it used to be the statue of Our Lady that we took for a walk.

I've been ringing the cathedral bells for sixty-three years now. I first became interested in bell ringing when I was a fire watcher during the war. Old Mr Rainford, who was head ringer for sixty-odd years, he took us up in the belfry and I said 'what's behind those doors?' He said eight bells. At the beginning of the war there was a ban on bell ringing until 1942. So as soon as they lifted the ban I learned along with Jimmy Glenn from the parish church. I've taught many a one since. We go bell ringing all over the place. I've rung all the bells round this area, I've lost count of all the churches I've rung bells in. Three hours and twenty minutes is the longest I've rung without stopping – 5,040 changes. When I'd been ringing for sixty years they presented a crystal bell to me. I thought we were having a do for the Queen

in the social centre but when I walked in they'd decorated it all for me. My honorary grandson, that's what I call him, John Rogan, is my Ringing Master now. I've taught him all I know and he takes over. I'm just a sort of figurehead now. I'm more-or-less the Tower Keeper.

The cathedral has always been a big part of my life. I do the guided tours, the collections, I looked after the social centre, I run a bingo on Wednesday nights for the bell fund, I help with the over sixties, and I've been involved with several of the youth clubs over the years. I got a Benemerenti medal ten years ago for service to the church. It's brought over by special envoy from the Pope. Three of us got it at the same time: Mrs Sweeney, who was Mayor of Lancaster many years ago, and Margaret Rainford who was on the council for many years. I started being an altar server from about eight and I'll be eighty this year and I've served the cathedral church ever since. Seventy-two years.

John Pye (b. 1925)

Westham Street Mission

We all went to Sunday school, to the Westham Street Mission on a Sunday afternoon. Me mother was glad to rid of us, she knew where you were. Mind you everybody did, they all went. We had harvest festivals, concerts, slides and all sorts, you know. It was well used. It was a Methodist mission. Mr and Mrs Matthews were in charge of it all and they were lovely people. They lived at Bowerham and they had a son. We used to go to Hest Bank a couple of times a year with the Methodists and we thought that was an occasion. That was all we got, you know. Times were different then. I still have a card from the Mission that I got on my first birthday, they gave all the children one.

Joan Varey, *née* Woodend (b. 1931)

Bridge Lane Mission

I left school at fourteen and went to work for Phil Barton who was a motorcycle engineer at the bottom of Bridge Lane. And I used to teach at the little mission down there; when I was a young lad I used to go and read lessons at the Bridge Lane Mission. It was a Sunday school and a small prayer place, it was Methodist. It was like the one that they had up Primrose, the Westham Street Mission.

Jack Watson (b. 1928)

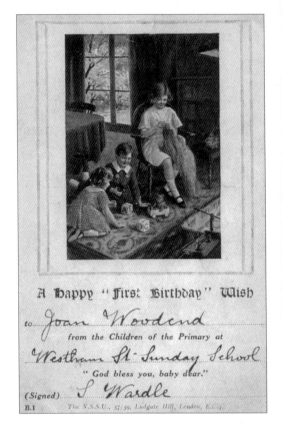

A happy "First Birthday" Wish

to *Joan Woodend*

from the Children of the Primary at

Westham St. Sunday School

" God bless you, baby dear."

(Signed) *S Wardle*

B.1   The N.S.S.U., 57/59, Ludgate Hill, London, E.C.4.

Right: A card from Westham Street Mission given to Joan Woodend on her first birthday, in 1932

Below: Phil Barton's garage at the bottom of Bridge Lane.

two

Homes and Neighbourhoods

'Poor but happy' times on Primrose

I was born in 1936. We moved onto Hope Street, Primrose when I was two and I lived there for the next sixty-five years. I grew up during the war. I was three years old when war broke out and my brother Stuart was only a baby. My dad went away in 1940 and we never saw him again till 1946. He got the Croix de Guerre. He wouldn't talk about it and we still don't really know how he got it but it was something to do with saving a wagon full of French men in North Africa. He was a POW and it was 1946 before he finally got home. Jim Bell, our neighbour, painted a great big banner 'Welcome Home Bob' and you've never seen anything as big in your life. We decorated the air-raid shelter with it for him coming home.

Dad was away all the time so consequently my mum had to work. She worked in the Co-op café and in the chippy at the end of the street for a while. My cousins next door, Harriet and Dorothy Till, used to see us off to school in a morning. And I think I had every illness under the sun, I must have cost my mother a fortune. I had measles, scarlet fever, yellow jaundice, chicken pox, I had everything. And everything had to be paid for. You used to pay so much a week in them days into a doctor's fund. I only threw doctor's bills away recently and there was one for four pound odd, for when I had measles. It was hard for the mothers, they all worked while their husbands were away at war.

I loved it growing up on Hope Street. It was happy times; poor but happy. You never

A Hope Street party celebrating the Coronation of George VI in 1937.

locked your door and everybody used to come in and out. You could leave your money on the sideboard with your book and the insurance man would just come in and collect it if you weren't around. You only locked your doors when you went to bed and even then everybody put their keys on a bit of string behind the letterbox in case anybody was coming in late.

Money was scarce, particularly during the war, and you used to borrow a bucket of coal if you ran out. Or you'd go and have one night in one house and they'd light their fire, and then another night in another house and they'd light theirs, to save coal, you know, and to save lighting. It was gas lighting; we didn't have electric till 1948, after my dad came home. And we had no bathrooms, just a tin bath in the yard that used to come in once a week. My mam used go across to Peel's and play cards and we went with her. Kids went everywhere with parents then. We used to go to Mrs Bell's a lot and they'd play cards or dominos, not for money 'cause they couldn't afford it, just to pass a night on. There was no telly, it was just radio.

We were a self-sufficient little area round Primrose. We had a chippy at one end of Hope Street and Herbie Brittain's grocers shop at the other end. At the bottom of Eastham Street hill on the right-hand side there was the Co-op, on the left-hand side there was Miss Shattock's chemist, and across the road was another grocer's shop, Whittle's; next door was a butcher's and at the end of Prospect Street, opposite the Park Hotel, was Rhodes' paper shop. Halfway along Prospect Street, on the top side, there was another chippy, Evelyn's, and further along was another little grocer's shop, Pape's. On the corner of Prospect Street and Primrose Hill there was another grocer's shop, Musgrove's: that was opposite the John O'Gaunt club which was on the other corner. On the bottom of Primrose Hill there was a

dairy where you bought milk straight out of the churns. And then on Clarence Street there was Wilson's bakery. It was quite self-sufficient really. You'd no need to go to town.

All the kids from other streets seemed to converge and play on Hope Street. The air-raid shelter was right outside Number 11, our house. We never had to go in the shelters, they just finished up as play areas. There were no cars on the street when we were kids. I think the first person to have a car on Hope Street was Ted Williams and his car and my husband Gordon's motorbike were the only two vehicles on Hope Street in the sixties. We played out on the streets but we were always in at quarter to seven at night. My mum used to come and shout: 'Come on kids, Dick Barton's on!' And everybody scattered and went in to their house to listen to Dick Barton Special Agent on the wireless.

Across the road, at Number 24, were the Cartlidges and he was a beautiful pianist. Mr Cartlidge organised a concert party that used to travel all the country villages during the war for entertainment. Jim Bell and Margaret Bell were in it, all the slightly older kids who were able to look after themselves, and they were called the Primrose Juveniles. It was any excuse for a party on the street, so we could dance. I loved dancing. I took dancing lessons on the top floor of the Collegian Club. It had the most gorgeous sprung floor, one of the nicest dance floors in town. I learned to dance up there in the late forties at classes run by Fred and Edna Patterson. We were noted for street parties and Mr Cartlidge used to play for us. They used to come from all over Lancaster to dance on Hope Street because he was such a brilliant pianist and the music was so good to dance to. We used to put soap powder on the street to make it slippier for dancing. He used to carry his piano outside the front door and put it on the street. The lads used to climb and sit on top of the air-raid shelter and watch all the lasses dancing. Me and Elaine Bush organised the last street party we had on Hope Street, for the Queen's Silver Jubilee in 1977.

I can probably remember all the families who lived on Hope Street when I was growing up. On the top side there were Chisholmes, Rileys, Sargents, McDowells, Greenalls, Fosters, Tills, Mrs Hodgon, Warings, Grace Crompton, Currys, Bells, Lowes, Wrights, Calverts, Clarkes, Battys, O'Hares and Jacksons. The bottom side was Kirbys, Leemings, Howards, Gardners, Grahams, Aldrens, Metcalfes, Gardners, Blezzards, Cartlidges, Smiths, Peels, Dowthwaites, Willans, Shorrocks, Simpsons, Proctors, Dobsons, Williams's, Marchments, Wildings, Whitesides, Armes's, Silverwoods, Woodhouses and Rileys.

Primrose was such a family orientated area but apart from only about nine Asian families, who I got on really well with, it's all students on Hope Street now. Everybody says it's not the same. You used to know everybody and I miss that community spirit. After I married my husband Gordon in 1962 we moved in with my parents and only left that house in 2003. When I was locking the front door of 11 Hope Street I cried. I was there sixty-five years and my husband lived there forty-two years. I still miss it, even though they were nearly all students when we left, there were still people round about. We live in a bungalow tucked in a corner and nobody passes. The only thing I don't miss about Hope Street is cleaning all the stairs!

Roberta Bateson, *née* Foster (b. 1936)

Dancing in the street

I was born on Prospect Street in 1933. Whenever there was something to celebrate they had all the parties and dances on Hope Street because it was great it was right flat and smooth and perfect for dancing. Oh it was fantastic. I mean we always went to Hope Street when the dances were on, at New Year and everything.

Gina Holden (b. 1933)

I was born in the parlour

I was born in Number 3 Hope Street, up Primrose. There was no rushing 'em to the infirmary in them days, I was born in the parlour, sitting room as they call it now but it was the parlour to us. If there was a confinement there was always someone to help out. One of the women on the street would come, like one of the old women, and they'd know what to do. And they'd either help till the midwife come or sometimes if the baby was due they'd deliver it before the midwife come. I remember seeing Mary Holmes at bingo and, God love her, she'd be ninety-one then and I was

Maureen Riley

in my sixties and she said: 'I remember holding you when you were born in your parlour.' She was there when I was born: 'And you haven't changed none!' she used to say. And if somebody died, you'd get one or two neighbours who were good at, as they called it, washing and laying them out. And they'd come, and if it was a lady that died and they hadn't a decent nightie, they'd bring a nightie as well and lay them out in that. The parlour was used for births and deaths. My mam, God rest her soul, died in our parlour when I was ten.

They were all good neighbours, it was lovely really up Primrose. There was always, you know, that togetherness. You were safe. You never locked your door till last thing at night. Whoever was last in they'd lock door. If you were going out you weren't frightened of leaving your door open. You used to always have a sideboard with a crocheted cover on it and you'd put your money for milkman under it. He'd just come in and take your money and that was it. Or you'd stick money for the insurance man under a book and he'd come in and take your money and write your book. And there was a feller used to come for the doctor's money as well. You could leave your doors open.

Monday was always washing day. We had a big boiler in the back kitchen and Dad used to light it before going out to work. The washing was done in there and you had a mangle in the back yard to wring them out. Then we used to have lines right across from our back door to the backs of Bradshaw Street. But you had to make sure you didn't have washing out if the midden men were coming. And we used to have a rack hanging from the ceiling in the living room, where there was a coal fire and it was always warm. And it used to have a pulley to pull it down, put the clothes on and then pull it back up. We used to scrub the doorstep and windowsill and right down the path and then donkey stone the doorstep

and windowsill. You'd put a bit of Lanry on it to fetch it white and then use your donkey stone down the sides and in front of the step. Everybody did it different. Some put donkey stone all over and some just on sides. Mansion polish was a red polish that some people put on their step but I think donkey stone looked better. Friday was black-leading and Brasso day. That was the day for black-leading the fireplace and polishing all the brass ornaments ready for the weekend.

Under the parlour window outside we used to have a flap and you lifted it up and the coalman dropped your bags of coal into the cellar through that. Then he'd leave his empty sacks outside and you'd come out to pay him and he'd show you how many sacks he'd emptied in. But you used to listen for how many he dropped to make sure it was the right number of sacks.

We didn't get electric lights put in till I was about fifteen or sixteen. And I can still remember my dad, he couldn't get over having lights at the bottom of the stairs and lights in the bedrooms and he kept switching them on and off. Before that we had gas lights but we only had one gas mantle in the parlour, one in the living room and one in the front bedroom. For the other rooms you had to have a candle to go to bed. The gas meter was down in the cellar and you put pennies in it. And the gas mantles were right fine and if they broke they were like dust. I was always going to Herbie Brittain's shop on the corner for them. That man had everything in that shop, from a mousetrap to a sliced loaf. And just down on Clarence Street there was this bakehouse, Alec Wilson's, where you'd go for pies and bread. You'd go and get two or three meat and potato pies for dinner and you'd take a jug with you and he'd fill it up with gravy. And the cakes and new-made bread coming out of the oven, oh they smelled lovely.

Maureen Deehan, *née* Riley (b. 1935)

Paddling and learning to knit in Skerton

I was born on Main Street, Skerton in 1926. I was the second eldest of four children and along with our parents we lived in the same house as my auntie and uncle and their three children until in 1935 our families moved into two brand new council houses next door to each other on Chestnut Grove on the Marsh. We lived on Main Street until I was nine and I have many childhood memories of Skerton. We used to go paddling on what we used to call the shards; on the ramparts there used to be a bit of a waterfall and we always used to paddle there. I remember getting a rusty nail through my foot once and my mother taking me to the infirmary. And on the shards there used to be a bloke who sawed woods and I can remember watching it all going round. There were houses near us in Skerton where all the gypsies used to live and in one house there used to be a lady who used to take kiddies in and learn them to knit. I think she was a bit of a dressmaker and when we were little you used to get these little celluloid dolls with moveable legs and arms, and she used to sell us bundles of cloth for a few pennies, that she used to have left over, and we used to make little dresses for our dolls.

Peggy Phillips, *née* Thomas (b.1926)

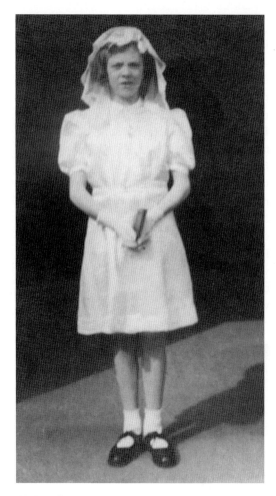

Marlene Campbell on her Confirmation day.

Donkeys, chickens and cows on Edward Street

I was born in 1932 in 1 St Mary's Parade, opposite the castle. When I was about three we went down on to Moor Lane, a big house opposite St Anne's church and I was there till I was about seven. Then we moved on to North Edward Street. None of it's there now. It was a big square cul-de-sac and we lived in the corner house at the top. You had to climb up fourteen steps to get to your front door. There was my mam and dad, and my grandma and grandad, and one of me aunties lived in that house up there. It was three storeys and we all lived there. I had another auntie and her husband across the road.

I can give you one funny story about a house on North Edward Street. Somebody sent for – I can't think what they were called then but it'd be the Environmental Health now – for the smell that used to come out of the house. And they came down, and this house had chickens in the bedroom and a donkey in the attic! I'd only be a child but I'll never forget them bringing that donkey down out of the attic. And then we moved onto South Edward Street when I was about nine, and my mum and dad and me got our own house then but my grandma and grandad lived next door but one.

I remember when I was young, I would never go out of the house when they used to take the cows to the auction market. They used to walk them all up in herds up South Edward Street, and there used to be a lot of them when they took them, maybe about fifty or so. The auction market wasn't where it is now, out of the way, it was somewhere round Thurnham Street near the canal. They'd do that about twice a week sometimes. The older people didn't bother but I used to keep indoors, I got a bit frightened because there was so many of them. You'd never take a herd of cows through the middle of town now would you?

My grandad was a right character. Everybody knew him: 'There's Bill Kay coming' they used to say. He was a poacher; he used to go and poach rabbits and he bred ferrets in the cellar. He took me once with him, he got me out of school and he took me rabbiting up Quernmore. He put the rabbit net over the hole and said 'Now I'm going back round there to put ferret in.' He said 'If a rabbit comes out, shout for me.' So I shouted 'Grandad there's a rabbit here.' And he shouted back 'Well wring its neck!' I started crying and I wouldn't do it. He never took me again because he lost his ferret. The rabbit went back down the hole and as soon as the ferret got the rabbit that was it, it didn't come back. 'Tha'll come wi' me no more!' he says. Oh he was a big poacher was my grandad. He got

Above left: Bill Kay knitting a fishing net in his Edward Street back yard.

Above right: Raymond and Malcolm Snape playing in the snow on the corner of Edward Street and Lodge Street in the early 1960s.

periwinkles from Morecambe as well and he used to knit fishing nets. He didn't go fishing, he just used to knit them for any fishermen that wanted to buy them. He taught me when I was about eight and I used to do a lot for him. If he was going into town he used to say, 'Do some o' that for me while I'm out,' and I used to sit there knitting away. You had a big woollen needle that had an eye but then another point going up in the middle of it, and you used to wrap your string round and round that and then somehow you knit it in squares, knotted it and then you did another line. You'd never see that now. I mean there's nowhere round here now they make string anyway. Where you come with a car round the back of Kingsway Baths, as if you're going down to North Road, there's a big garage on the corner isn't there? Well there used to be a small place there, right on the corner, where they used to make string. Grandad used to go there for all his string.

I went to St Anne's School, that's not there any more either. It was on Edward Street, on the opposite side of the road to where we lived. I'd only to walk across the road. I always went home for my dinner. When I was eleven I went to St Thomas's School on Marton Street. I can always remember when I used to go to school at St Thomas's, my grandma used to give me money and say: 'Now don't lose that and when you're on your way home call at the butcher's.' And I had to get either some stewing steak or a rabbit from the butcher's that was on the corner of Brewery Lane. People ate a lot of rabbit then, rabbit pie was lovely, but I don't think I'd eat rabbit now. But my grandad used to eat sheep's head, and tripe. On Nicholas Street, there was two tripe shops and he'd go down there every morning and tie his scarf round the shop handle, come home, light the fire, have a cup of tea and his breakfast, and then go back and stand at the beginning of the queue. And all the women used to say 'Hey, there's a queue here!' He'd say 'I know, I've been once, that's my scarf.' One was better than the other but they soon sold out, both of these tripe shops, so that's why he used to go at seven every morning and put his scarf round the handle.

I remember there used to be a toffee shop on the corner of Lodge Street and Edward Street, that was called Lynam's, and there was also a sweetshop on Alfred Street. At the other end of Alfred Street there was a big selling-out shop, they call them off-licences now, and there was a laundry on there as well, Alfred Street Laundry. They used to come and pick laundry up and then bring it back to you when it was finished. There was a big Co-op on South Edward Street that was really handy. And down Lodge Street there used to be a slipper factory where they made slippers. Everything's changed round there now, there's no houses or nothing.

Marlene Snape, *née* Campbell (b. 1932)

Dad started using the front room on Briery Street as a dairy

We lived on Briery Street when we moved from Shap to Lancaster in 1930. There was always plenty to do there when I was a lad. At nights in summertime, me and my mate Albert Barber, we used to go in a little flat boat down on the river and come back with the tide. We were nine or ten year old then. A lot of people used to go out on boats on the Lune. The Prestons, who lived on Briery Street, they had boats on the river. My dad started using the front room at Briery Street as a dairy. In a morning he used to walk to Aldcliffe and milk cows for a bloke, then he'd come back and get his breakfast and go to work at Pye's. He started getting milk off this bloke and I used to deliver 70 gallons a day for him, all round the Marsh and Sibsey Street. And it was all tipping it out then, no bottles. I used to have

The Preston brothers, of Briery Street, building a boat on Long Marsh Lane.

a truck, a bogey, on wheels and I used to pour milk from the big churn into smaller cans and I'd get the milk out of these with measures. My dad had about 40 hens and ducks up near Furness Street and I used to take eggs on my rounds as well and my mother used to make butter and cream and I had to sell it. We used to go to the cricket field on a Sunday, to the tennis players, and take milk for them and cream for the strawberries and cream. When I was finishing school my dad said that I could have the milk round but I said I didn't want it! He had an allotment as well that he used to go down to when he'd finished work at night. He used to grow all his own vegetables.

When I was eleven, we moved onto West Road to a bigger house and I went to Dallas Road School. That's where I learned the bad habit of smoking. When we went past Castle Station there was a machine where, for a penny, you got two Churchman Number Ones and two matches. So we used to have one at dinnertime and one in the afternoon before we came home. We used to live in 36 West Road. There was Ada Sowden's shop – her brother was Charlie Sowden, he used to deliver fruit down to her. She was married to a bloke from Borwick, somewhere like that, when she was younger. Then there was a passageway, then I forget who lived in that first house, then there was the Clarkes – she had a parrot, she used to put it on a stand outside and when they were all coming up from Williamson's it used to whistle at these lasses coming up. Next door to that was ours, Number 36, and then it was Mrs Banks next door and then it was Westfield House then. I never did know the people in Westfield House because they were the 'high and mighty' as you would call it then. They looked after all Westfield Village and they kept themselves well and truly away from us.

And down on the Marsh when I was young:

where the Marsh Estate is now there used to be allotments down one side and down the other side, down Willow Lane side, at the side of the Co-op, we built a Scout hut in the corner of the field there. We used to go there, Scouts and Cubs, on Wednesday nights I think. Whittaker's Field, as they called it, was where they later built all the Marsh Estate houses, you got the Scout hut, the Co-op, then there was St George's Mission, then there was the field, and then there was the school, and then there was fields again until you got to the allotments further down at the bottom of Coverdale Road. I've spent some hours on that field.

We used to spend Saturday mornings sitting on the swings eating pies from Pilkington's. I used to like their butter pies best, they were lovely. Hughie Pilkington used to run the post office when I was there and they had a bakehouse there as well.

And when the tomatoes were out we used to put our arms through the fence, because you used to get panes knocked out of greenhouses, we used to put our hands through and just manage to get tomatoes out. Across the road from the post office, Jimmy Downham used to live. He was a big noise in the Lads Club, he used to do a helluva lot for the Lads Club did Jimmy Downham. He was a right character was Jimmy Downham, a grand bloke.

Bill Stockdale (b. 1923)

You have to be old to know where Monmouth Street was

I was born in 1927 on Monmouth Street. My dad was Jimmy Wilson and my mam was Clara and I had six sisters. You have to be old to know where Monmouth Street was. You know St Peter's church? Well just as you start to go up the hill there's Bulk Street on the left, and then there's a car park – that's Monmouth Street. On the other side, there's the big car

park which was Billy Sticks's iron yard and we used to play in there as kids. There was a chap, his name was Carter, and he had a stable down there. He had a horse and cart and he also had a hearse. You got free toys on Easter Monday and he always used to take the toys down to the Easter Field. He'd give us a lift down and he used to say 'Sit there and don't move.' He was a lovely man. I moved onto Rowan Place on the Marsh when I was twelve, when they knocked Monmouth Street down.

Ralph Wilson (b. 1927)

Playing football with a pig's bladder on Boundary Road

I was born in 1920 on Boundary Road, where the Pointer roundabout is now. There were seven of us children and my father worked at the shipyard, Lune Mills. Although the houses have gone my playing area, the street I lived on, is still there. Railway Street's still standing and the backyards of Railway Street were on Boundary Road. That's where we would play football, mostly in bare feet, and they weren't stone bricks they were slate bricks. I go and have a look occasionally; the houses have gone but the slates I played football on, barefooted with a rag ball or a pig's bladder, are still there. We'd go down to the auction and get a pig's bladder. Then you'd to get an old pipe stem from one o' the neighbours who smoked a pipe, put it in the bladder and blow it with your mouth. Oh, it was hard work to blow a bladder up and they stunk!

Jimmy Downham (b. 1920)

It was all different then round China Street and Covell Cross

Dad took a job as a steward at the John O'Gaunt Club on Prospect Street. Then he applied to Mitchell's and we moved into the Black Bull on China Street in 1938. It's

Above: St Mary's Place, off Church Street, in 1927.

Right: Best pals Jimmy Stewart, Jack Watson and Billy Butler in the late 1930s.

changed name and it's now called the Duke of Lancaster. At that time I was in my last year at Scotforth School. I spent me last year at Scotforth School not knowing many people down on China Street. And then as time got on I got talking to Jimmy Stewart and we started mating round together and going to different places and then we met Billy Butler on the other side and we became firm pals, we used to go everywhere together. Billy Butler lived on St Mary's Parade and Jimmy lived in a lodging house on Castle Hill that his mother and father had. She had about twenty or so Irish navvies staying there. And they used to have these beds and she used to charge I think about ten pence or so for the night. And they used to have a bowl of soup, or a bowl of broth

or whatever you call it and a bed for the night. And that's how she made her living.

It was all different then round China Street and Covell Cross. Where Mitre House is now, there was a big building with an alleyway down, and stables, behind that were bowling greens and we used to go 'lorching'. Do you know what lorching is? Pinching apples. They come and caught us one day and I sprained me ankle as I jumped off the wall, it was about fifteen foot drop. Bridge Lane was there but there was no road down to the bus station then. There was a little alleyway by the Judges' lodgings to go down to St Mary's Place and there must have been thirty or forty houses down there. The Thompsons, they're big families in Lancaster, and the Coultons, they lived all round there. Then we got pally with the Wilsons, the Coultons, the Thompsons, the Longhorns and the Jacksons. We all used to play around the cross in front of the Judges' lodgings. We'd play games like Kiss, Tap and Torture. You either could kiss the girl, or you had a tap, or you got your arm twisted for torture.

Jack Watson (b. 1928)

Out with the old, in with the new: from back to back houses to council estates

I worked for fifty-four years in the building trade from 1927 to 1981. I started working for Frank Moore & Co. after leaving Lancaster Royal Grammar School at sixteen and I retired as director of Heysham Building Co. when I was seventy. In my first job after leaving school, working for Frank Moore & Co. I remember working on slum clearances. In 1928 we demolished some of the old slums in the centre of town, round the St Leonardgate area. There were lots of small terraced two-up two-down-type houses and the worst of them only had one tap between four houses. They were building a lot of new council housing then.

In 1930 I was a nineteen-year-old trainee working for Nicholson and Wright on the building of the Ryelands Estate. One of my jobs was to show people into their new houses when they were available and show them how to work the boilers etcetera. A lot of the ladies had tears in their eyes. They were so pleased, they almost tried to kiss me and I was only nineteen! They said 'Wait till I show my husband this house, it's lovely.' We built about a hundred three- and four-bedroom houses and they averaged about £300 each to build. In those days a bricklayer got about £3 10s and a labourer got £2 15s a week. I got about 15 shillings. I was still working for Nicholson and Wright when they began building the Marsh Estate in about 1934. I remember that some of the first houses that we

built had to be evacuated for a while to deal with cockroaches. We built fifty houses a year, about a hundred on Ryelands and a hundred on the Marsh. During my years I worked on building most of Lancaster's council estates. I worked on the building of houses at Bowerham, Beaumont Bridge, Halton Road. We built the shopping area on Ryelands and the Co-op and in the 1950s and '60s my own firm, Heysham Building Co., built the Ridge shops.

John H. Taylor (b. 1911)

From Blue Anchor Lane to the Marsh Estate

We were born in Blue Anchor Lane, Market Square. I think there was about eight houses there. Four where we lived, we lived in the middle, and one shared toilet between four houses. And the other toilet was for the other four families. And they used to take turns in scrubbing it. Because I can remember me mother used to scrub it down. We used to have the newspaper on string. Our house on Blue Anchor Lane was the middle one and it used to have a big window just like a shop. Jean and Mary Riley were our neighbours on there, and the Harpers and Lennons. And then down Chancery Lane was the Hennedys.

I was about seven or eight when we moved from there down into 40 Chestnut Grove in 1935. My Granny and Grandad Ginocchio, they were on opposite side at Number 11 Chestnut Grove. Me Auntie Lizzie Hennedy, me mam's sister, she was at 50 Chestnut Grove. And me other auntie, Stirzaker, went on Cedar Road… There were three sisters all living near… 40 Chestnut Grove had three bedrooms. They were all black-leaded fires in the living rooms. But they were nice, they were kept shining. And they had a top over the oven and we used to keep our nighties in there and they used to be nice and warm for bed. I used to put me curlers in there as well.

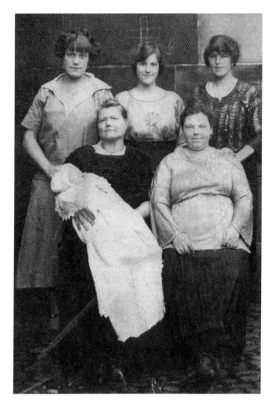

Joan and Betty Hargreaves' Granny Ginocchio with her four daughters: Marie (Joan and Betty's mother), Lizzie, Jane and Sarah, and baby Michael Baker, pictured in Golden Ball Yard, off Market Square.

Only thing was, the toilet was downstairs and you used to have to come down. Mind you, everybody used to have 'Gerrys' didn't they? Buckets, and empty it!

Grandad Ginocchio was my mam's dad and they'd moved from Blue Anchor Lane. Grandad Ginocchio went to Chestnut Grove, we went to Chestnut Grove, Lizzie did, and Aunt Sarah went to Cedar Road. Grandad, Anthony Ginocchio, worked at Williamson's. He was called Anthony but they used to call him Sorry Ginocchio. And he never ever wore shoes, he wore clogs. Every Sunday, Grandad used to sit near the window on Chestnut Grove and I'd trim his moustache. He used to play the jaws harp as well… There was no cars. We used to play marbles, alleys, in the gutter.

I used to have a drawer full of alleys and we used to swap our best ones…

When anybody died, my mum would take us to see them laid out. It always had that funny smell of white lilies. And I always remember, they used to do this then, my mam would say 'touch them then you won't dream about them' and I never wanted to do this. And do you know, I couldn't stop dreaming about them! When they died, they used to put a penny on their eye, to keep their eyelids closed, and usually a thing tied up or a pillow under their chin… My granny, she always wore a white pinny, and she laid people out. When she died, Mrs Wootton took over laying people out on Chestnut Grove. Every street had someone to lay people out, you know.

Betty Cummings and Joan Herman, *née* Hargreaves

The Marsh Estate's unpaid district nurse

Anybody that was badly, old Nana Wootton was there. She was like unpaid district nurse was that woman, if anybody deserved a medal she did. When our Betty was badly, me mother said: 'Nip up and get Nana Wootton.' If any of us kids cut ourselves badly, she'd know what to do, Nana Wootton. It didn't matter what time of day you went, if she was making dinner or what, she'd stop what she was doing and come. She used to wash and lay 'em out when they were dead.

Ken Lambert (b. 1929)

Nana Wootton was with me when my kiddies were born, all four of them, and she was great. You had neighbours who were midwives then. She wasn't a qualified nurse or anything, she was just there. She either held your hand or wiped your brow, you know. As long as you

'Nana' Wootton with husband Stan, daughter Delta and son Stan.

had a basin and a big jug, you'd get your water in a big dish and she used to wash them. She did everything, she even used to bring you a meal. You used to be in bed ten days in them days. You used to be wobbly coming downstairs, your legs were that weak! Nowadays I think they nearly chuck you out of hospital after a day, don't they?

Peggy Phillips, *née* Thomas, (b. 1926)

The Council Housing Officer

Miss Baines, she was a really old biddy, she was. She was the housing officer and everybody did exactly what she said. She used to come round every Monday, to the house, and go through every house. I mean there weren't as many houses on Marsh then as there is now, there were no like bungalows, it was just the estate… She used to come round every Monday morning but you didn't know what time. She used to go right through the house from top to bottom. If it was dirty you got

a warning: 'Get it cleaned up or else you're out!'

She would go round your house, she'd look at your sink and everything, your floors to see if they were clean. She even looked at your beds. I mean, it was a joke on the estate at one time that on a Sunday everybody had their washing out on the line. 'Cause maybe they only had one pair of sheets for beds and they used to do all their washing on a Sunday and put 'em all on beds, you see. Kids couldn't sleep in beds on a Sunday night 'cause they had to keep 'em clean, you know. But she went round every week, and there was no excuse – she had the right to come in! You know, you couldn't say 'no, you're not coming in' or you'd be out. I always remember me mam saying that she come one Monday and me dad never used to work nights but they'd had a big order on at Williamson's and he'd worked nights and he was in bed. And she come round and she said: 'Well I'll go upstairs.' And me mother said: 'Well you can go up but he's in bed; he's been on nights.' She said: 'You're alright, I won't be getting in with him.' She still went up! Yeah, she still went in the bedroom and me dad was in bed.

Any wrongdoings in the house or anything like that, you know, she was there. You couldn't have a house unless you was married – you had to have a marriage certificate. Oh yeah, nobody could have a house unless you was married; you had to have a marriage certificate before you got a house. Oh yeah, you had to show your marriage certificate. If you had one child you only got a two-bedroomed house. If you had different sets you got [more bedrooms] to accommodate you, you know. 'Cause me mam and dad were one of the first people to live in Number 8 Sycamore, and what really used to annoy me mum was that it was a really big back double bedroom, it had two windows, you know. And during the war they put a board in between it, so you could take evacuees. Then, when I got to the age of about seven, we already had the board up and we used it as three bedrooms. And she came, she used to keep a check, and she says to him 'you have to move out now, you've got to go to 58 Cedar Road.' They gave you no choice: 'There's a three-bedroomed at 58 Cedar.' Me dad said to her: 'We don't really want to move, we're alright here.' She said 'You've got one boy, you've got one girl but you're in a two-bedroomed house. Sorry but you'll have to get out. If you don't take that house you're out! No second chances or anything, 'cause it's illegal to have two children in one [bedroom].' Me dad says to her: 'Well what about when evacuees were here?' She said: 'Oh, everybody did different things then but it's not allowed now.' And they had to move… Where she said, you had to go! You had no choice.

It was same as if you were on waiting list for a house: if a house came empty … you were told: 'You either take that house or you go right back down to the bottom of the waiting list.' If you refused a house you went right down to the bottom of the waiting list and there was no way you'd get a house in between. You couldn't [object], she was the boss and that was it.

Maureen Palwankar, *née* Schofield (b. 1942)

She was a good housing manager. We moved from Skerton to Ryelands and we had to have our beds stoved [fumigated]. If your house wasn't clean, you'd get two weeks to clean it or you were out. As I say, when we first went on, you know, Ryelands was absolutely the tops. They used to put their name down for Ryelands, they couldn't get on Ryelands. She didn't knock, she just used to walk in, and give you a certain time to clean up otherwise you were evicted. Couples had to have a marriage

New houses on Chestnut Grove on the Marsh Estate in the late 1930s.

certificate to get a house as well. She was fearless. Even though we were poor we were always clean. There was no rent arrears then – she collected the rents as well.

Audrey Entwistle, *née* Bleasdale (b. 1928)

Your house was clean when she was around. Everybody was frightened of her. Your gardens and hedges even had to be perfect.

Gwen Bell, *née* Hewitt (b. 1930)

Good neighbours

I moved into 10 Rowan Place in 1959. Nobody had anything, which was good, one neighbour helped the other neighbour. Washing machines you'd hire, and we'd all have a laugh over that … If you got it on a Monday they'd take it back Tuesday but if you got it on the Friday you could keep it all weekend, so that meant somebody else could borrow the washer … nobody had automatic washers or anything like that … it was like a small electric [washing machine] with a hand wringer. And then, as time got on, then you got one with the automatic wringer … a fella brought them and picked them up … There was an old boiler, when I first got the house… a cast iron boiler, in the kitchen, where you could boil the clothes. You had the black lead fireplace, and then in time you changed it and had so much put on your rent so's you could get the tiled fireplace. For a tiled fireplace, with the hearth and the two like things put out at the side for an ornament, you paid so much on your rent for that. It was like the bathrooms, you didn't have a sink in your bathroom: you had a toilet and you had a bath, but you didn't have a sink. So you paid so much extra [rent] and had some of your bathroom cupboard took out for to have a little sink put in. I knew none o' the neighbours when I first come here, but they were good, Mrs Broughton and all them, Emily Rowan, Cunninghams, Barbara Carr, they were all just like yourself: nobody had nothing, down-to-earth, everybody helped one another… 'cause you could trust everybody, couldn't ye? Nobody done any harm to one another.

Patsy Cuffe (b. 1940)

Still good neighbours: Cliff Akister, Maureen Deehan, Patsy Cuffe and Lillian Hennedy, Chestnut Grove, 2002.

A Skerton School classroom, c.1930. David Varey is the first boy seated on the left of the picture in the front row.

Boys from St Peter's Roman Catholic Junior School in 1934. From left to right, back row: Laurence Bonnell, -?-, Bill Hodkinson, James Taylor, Dennis Walmsley, Bob Howson. Centre row: Norman Baker (?), Alan Tennant, Ernie Atkinson, Tommy Tindall, Albert Gaskell, Jim Maudsley, Arthur Ronnigan. Front row: -?-, -?-, Tony Macari, Leo Campbell, Ralph Wilson, -?-, Joe Richmond.

St Peter's School playground in 1947.

Clarendon Terrace in Skerton decked out for Queen Elizabeth II's Coronation in 1953

Briery Street residents in a procession to celebrate the Coronation of Elizabeth II in 1953.

A Coronation party on Main Street in Skerton, 1953.

three

Wartime

Painting seams on big sisters' legs

I was ten when the war started. I had two older sisters and during the war they couldn't get hold of silk stockings or nylons. I remember them putting gravy browning on their legs before they went out at night and then they used to stand on a stool and I had to paint a black line down the back of their legs to make it look like the seam of a stocking. I remember the ARP blokes guarding Carlisle Bridge. They used to train the ARP wardens on St George's Quay but they didn't have rifles, they used to march with broomsticks on their shoulders. As kids we used to tease them.

Ken Lambert in 1947.

We lived on Chestnut Grove on the Marsh and there was an air-raid shelter in a field that we used to call 'the cabbage patch'. It's where they've built Willow Nursery School now. When the siren used to go my mother would take us three kids to the shelter but if my father was in bed he wouldn't get up and go to the shelter, he stayed in bed. They were still finishing building the Marsh Estate then and we used to run errands for the workmen. They always wanted ten Woodbines but to be able to buy Woodbines, you had to buy ten Pashas as well. Pashas were awful cigarettes that stank but the workmen used to give us the Pashas for going to the shop for them. Other cigarettes available then were Kensitas and they used to have four extra on the end of the packet with the words 'Four for your friends'. And the workmen also used to give us those four for going for them.

Ken Lambert (b. 1929)

Throwing hand grenades at Quernmore

My dad was a sergeant-major in the Home Guard during the war. He spent most of his time guarding Carlisle Bridge and Ashton Hall. Of a Sunday, they used to go out in wagons up Quernmore and they used to have drills, throwing live hand grenades in trenches. They used to have regular army officers there making sure they were doing the right thing, so there was no accidents. But most of their time was spent on doing guard duties.

Bill Stockdale (b. 1923)

Your gas mask had to go too

Wherever you went, your gas mask had to go too! At school, it was worse than forgetting your homework to leave your gas mask at home. Teacher would check everyday and you were sent home straight away to collect it, with a severe reprimand. We had shelters

Children at Scotforth School, c.1940. Marlene Ellwood is kneeling second left on the second row.

in the school yard and once a week we had practice, like the schools now have fire practice. Also, once a week, we had to put on our gas mask and teacher would come round and put what I think was a piece of paper on the bottom of the mask: if that stuck then everything was okay. The air raids were usually at night. My father was in a reserved occupation: his job was charge nurse at the mental hospital, a job he was totally dedicated to. He was a wonderful husband, father, nurse and friend. He had a shelter built below ground in our garden, so he could leave us safe whilst he got on his bike to go to help look after his men at the hospital.

I had an older sister Joan, older brother, Fred, and in 1944, a younger brother Danny, but the war years were mainly the three of us older children. My mother was the youngest mum in our cul-de-sac so she was asked to be the fire warden. This meant we had a card in the sitting room window and we had the stirrup pump in case of fire. Two older retired men were the ARP wardens, with tin hats. During an air raid they would patrol their area and, I remember, they would come in our shelter and call out 'Everything okay Mrs Ellwood?' Mum would reply and off they would go to the next shelter. Lots of people

had Anderson shelters in their sitting rooms. I used to be scared when we could hear the planes going over. They only used Lancaster as a marker for bombing Barrow shipyard, so we were lucky; it must have been terrible in the places that got bombed every night. The blackout was a nightmare. You had to have this horrible black material at the windows and you had to turn off the lights in the kitchens or hall before you could open the back or front doors. If you forgot, and I never quite understood how this happened, you would hear a really loud voice shouting 'Put that light out!' When anyone came to the door you had to make sure all lights were out and of course there were no street lights allowed.

I remember the evacuees being brought around the street in a crocodile-like line. My mum took one boy in and he stayed quite a while until his parents wanted him home. Rationing was a problem but my dad came off farming stock so we could get a little help at times. When I was playing out my mum used to say 'Watch for the Co-op truck coming to the shop.' Then we would all run in and our mums would go to see what had arrived. Of course the truck was horse-drawn, as was the dustbin cart and many more. We used to have egg powder that you could make omelettes

Evacuees from Salford outside Greaves School, 1 September 1939.

with but I didn't like it, it was horrid stuff. Sweets were in short supply, plus we had to have coupons to buy them, but a little shop near our school used to make parched peas – hot if you were lucky, cold if you were not. Also, at the Co-op, once in a while we could get a small bag of cocoa powder with some sort of sweetener in. You would wet your finger and then dip it in the bag. Bananas were few and far between and a real treat but they were only available on a child's blue ration book. I remember having to go on Saturdays to the bakery and queuing very early in the morning to get bread and a few small cakes. The first people there got the best choice but you were only allowed a few.

One of the slogans during wartime was 'Dig for Victory' and everyone was expected to dig up their gardens and plant potatoes and vegetables. Even the front gardens were dug up and planted. We had fruit trees in our garden and mum would wrap some of the individual fruits up in newspaper and keep them in an old tin

trunk till Christmas. The parks all had their railings taken down to be used for the war effort but they were never replaced after the war.

Due to young men having to go to war, schools and shops, offices, hospitals, every walk of life, were short of a workforce so in some places they let married ladies come back, where before the war when they got married they stayed at home. This happened at Scotforth School, we got some teachers back who had left to get married. Due to all the evacuees coming to our school, we only went to school in the mornings and went to a church hall in the afternoons to play games organised by helpers.

Lots of people were evacuated here from Coventry, which was badly bombed, and they worked at a munitions factory in town. A lot of them stayed after the war and are still here today. My in-laws worked at the munitions factory on night and day shifts from six till six. My husband used to say he was one of the first 'latch-key kids'. When the war was over the street parties were great fun. Everyone was welcome and people would take their tables and chairs out on the street. Mums would provide food: jam and paste sandwiches, jelly and cakes. The street was decorated with bunting and someone would provide music.

Marlene Russell, *née* Ellwood (b. 1933)

Lancaster virtually had no cars at all

When the war broke out it was sad really because we started losing all the lads from around. My brother went in the RAF, one of my sisters went in munitions and one went up to the County Mental Hospital to work. I was the youngest of the lot. My dad was an ARP warden. I went to Greaves School early on in the war and of course we lost all our teachers because they all went in the forces. So we were taught by the older teachers who had come back from retirement. And we never did any lessons hardly because they used to say there's a teacher off today and we just had to go and 'dig for victory' down at the back of the school and put potatoes in. There were no cars on the road because you couldn't get petrol unless you were an emergency service or a doctor, things like that. Lancaster virtually had no cars at all. And I can always remember Barrow being bombed: because the aeroplanes used to come in from Germany very heavy and droning and they used to head for Williamson's Park memorial, and then turn at Williamson's Park and go over to Barrow. And you could hear Barrow being thumped with the bombs. And then you could hear them coming back, lightly loaded, droning away in the distance. And all the barrage balloons right round Barrow. We went up by St Mary's church on the top, the priory church, and we could actually see all the sky lit up across the bay at Barrow. As the war finished the family all got back together and all went back to normal really.

Jack Watson (b. 1928)

Bombs at Bowerham Barracks and the mental hospital

My father was a male nurse at Lancaster County Mental Hospital when war broke out, and he was in a reserved occupation because of his job. The sad thing was, often they were handed a white feather but someone had to stay behind and care for the patients.

We didn't come off badly in Lancaster. We did hear the sirens go but it was usually because the bombers were heading for Barrow dockyards etcetera. One night they did drop bombs on Bowerham Barracks and at the mental hospital but most people thought it was an error: that they mistook it for Barrow.

Everywhere we went we had to carry our gas masks, it was like ladies carrying a handbag. Babies had a very big gas mask which went completely over them and children had a Mickey Mouse type gas mask. The whole area of Lancaster, everywhere, was in total darkness at night, complete blackout. There were no lights showing from your home and no street lights. Of course everything was rationed and you had food and clothing coupons. You couldn't buy stockings so we used to buy lotion in a bottle to rub some colour on our legs; some even used gravy browning and if you had a steady hand you used to draw a line down the back of your leg to look like a seam. Often, if people heard of a shop having

An unexploded bomb in the grounds of the Moor Hospital during the Second World War.

a delivery of certain hard-to-get foods, a big long queue would appear very quickly.

In Queen Street, I can't just remember whereabouts, was an ammunitions factory and workers came to stay here from Coventry. In part of Waring and Gillows on North Road they made glider parts, mainly the wings. I had to leave my job and I went there on nights, helping to make up the plywood. All, or most, of it was shipped over from Canada. The Midland Hotel on the promenade at Morecambe was taken over as a hospital for the wounded soldiers, sailors and airmen who had been injured in battle. They would be pushed out onto the verandah in their beds to get the sea air.

The fun side of life during the war was that at Morecambe dance halls we always had lots of partners to dance with because soldiers and airmen were billeted around Bowerham Barracks (which is now St Martin's College) and Halton Camp was used as a TA camp for square-bashing for airmen in Morecambe.

Joan Kimpton, *née* Ellwood (b. 1925)

Fighting Hitler on the Marsh
One of me earliest memories: I was getting ready for school, about eightish and the radio was on, you know, morning news in wartime. And this man come on reading the news, and he said summat about Hitler marched into Poland... And me and me sister's getting ready for school – and me dad was a motor engineer like, and he was often doing jobs at home. And he had this big soldering iron, he'd been soldering... I picked this thing up and I said to me mother, 'If Hitler come in here now mother I'd get him on 'ead with this soldering iron', And I went like that – well the flipping iron was about this big – was 'ead of it. It was a whacking thing. Big copper head. Well it went like a rocket through lounge window into backyard. And I was left with wooden handle! Me mother says, 'Well I don't know about Adolf Hitler son, but your father will have summat to say when he comes in.' And because it was wartime we couldn't get any glass, so me dad took, took a picture off the wall and took the glass out of it. And he tacked it in over the hole. And it had to stop like that all through the war. Where Marsh Infants School is now, that was cabbage patch. We played soccer on there... Right on the front. It was open ground that... Between Mrs Winder's old house there and Milking Stile Lane it was open ground... So all the wartime we played on there. We attacked Hitler and everybody on there. We dug trenches galore. We could have dug for Wimpey's. And over the back by the air-raid shelter, up against Westfield, they had allotments then in wartime. But then later on ... they finished with allotments and all the elder lads, the big lads, they dug a massive pit. And then they got railway sleepers and things and put turf over it. And that was an absolutely magnificent den. You could have got half the Marsh in it.

Jack Hurtley

The war will be over and finished before you get called up!'
I left school just before my fourteenth birthday and I started work at Williamson's and then I went to work for a biscuit firm, McVitie and Price's. They used to have a garage, where they've built the new flats on the quay, and they used to deliver the skips of biscuits to the station and we used to have to unload them, sort them out, and deliver them round Cumbria, the Fylde, all over the place. I got to know the Lake District doing that. I worked at the grammar school after that, as a lab assistant and caretaker, till I got called up in 1943.

I was a signalman in the Royal Navy. I was on the D-Day landings and then I went across France, Belgium and Holland. A priest came

John Pye aboard HMS *Indomitable*, Malta, 1946.

Sinking the Bismarck

In 1937 I joined the Navy, after being made redundant from Seward's Heating Engineers on Market Street. I did nine years active service and three years reserve. After training at Chatham I was drafted to HMS *Imogen*. The Spanish Civil War was on and the *Imogen*, in company with HMS *Hood*, patrolled the east coast of Spain. We looked after the interests of British nationals in Spain, giving them protection and, when necessary, we evacuated them and took them down to Gibraltar. Then World War Two broke out on 3 September 1939 and for the next six months I was out in the Atlantic hunting U-boats. In that six months the *Imogen* sunk two submarines.

In 1940 I changed ships and joined HMS *Sheffield*. Together with HMS *Glasgow* we went to Norway because the Norwegian campaign had started. Then the *Sheffield*, with *Ark Royal* and HMS *Renown*, joined Force H at Gibraltar. We were coming back from Malta and we got word to deploy to the UK with all dispatch because the *Bismarck* had got out of the Baltic Sea. We had to come up from Gibraltar through the Bay of Biscay in terrible weather, and as we were on our way up we heard the bad news that HMS *Hood* had been blown to bits by *Bismarck*. Everybody was shattered because the *Hood* was the pride of the British Navy. The *Sheffield* was sent to find the *Bismarck* but keep well out of her way because we were only 10,000 tons, she would have made a meal of us. We found her but we were nearly all killed by a strike force of torpedo bomber planes from the *Ark Royal* who mistook us for the *Bismarck*. Fortunately the *Sheffield* was not hit before they realised who we were. They loaded up a second time and this time they got two hits on the *Bismarck*, damaging the rudder so she couldn't steer. We were sending signals back and ships within a thousand miles were racing. The next thing we heard from the admiral was '*Sheffield* keep out

aboard our ship and he was saying Mass and I started answering. He said 'We've got an altar boy somewhere.' So I became his altar boy through France, Germany and Holland and every time he came I served Mass for him. The chaplain was Father Holland, who later became Bishop of Salford. I went out to Malta in 1946 on HMS *Indomitable*. During the war, when I was delivering biscuits, we used to go to Barrow Dockyard and there was two ships being built – *Indomitable* and *Indefatigable* – and I said I'd love to go on one of them. My boss said 'John, the war will be over and finished before you get called up.' But that's the ship I went out on to Malta – *Indomitable*. After I was demobbed, I came back and worked at Storey's for thirty-eight years till I was made redundant. Then I worked at the Moor Hospital for about six years till I retired.

John Pye (b. 1925)

Above left: Leading Seaman Charlie Adams, 1939.

Above right: Charlie Adams at an HMS *Sheffield* Flag Day in Sheffield town centre, 1996.

of the way: the big lads are coming.' And they got in a certain position to the west and they all fired on her. The destroyers picked about a hundred survivors up but they had to get out when a signal came that U-boats were coming to help the *Bismarck*. Nearly two thousand died that morning. Churchill was delighted that we'd sunk the *Bismarck*.

The war finished in August 1945 and Charlie came out. You all had a number, a demob number. I came out of active service at the beginning of 1946. I couldn't wait to get down to the Giant Axe to watch football again... Went to work for the council in Marton Street Yard, where the magistrate's court is now, as a store keeper. My dad said 'Get yourself a job because they'll all be coming home now...' After about fifteen years I transferred to the water department, the Lune Valley Water Board which became the North West Water Board. I got a desk job there as a technical clerk and I was there till I retired in 1982.

Charlie Adams (b. 1917)

Four

Working Lives

The Moor Hospital

I started working at the Moor Hospital in 1938 when I was eighteen. Well when I first started there, in those days the females were called nurses and the males were called attendants. And of course as years went on, as people qualified, we became nurses. So literally, when I first started I was an attendant and when I retired I was senior nursing officer. Course in this time, in the intervening years, I got the studying: SRN, RMN, RMPA. Then of course, like everything else, you move on and on into administration. That's it.

In the early years, from 1938, I can only talk about the male wards, reason being because the male wards and the female wards was a no-go area. There was the North End of the hospital and there was the South End. South End was females, North End was males. They never mixed, apart from on Thursday night. Thursday night in winter was the dance night. Oh it was fun for patients and staff. Course in those days we had our own orchestra. Not a band – orchestra! You could have anything up to twenty or thirty players. They were all staff. In actual fact, the bandmaster, the last one, George Morris, he was a saxophonist, a wonderful player. You mention it and we had it! Oh yes, we had everything. We had what today would have been professional footballers, because quite a number of them who played football wanted such as the Liverpools and the Manchesters to sign them up. Cricket was county cricket standard. Oh yes! The staff football teams played against such teams as Everton 'A' team, Liverpool 'A' team, in a very good league. The cricket side played against a lot of East Lancashire teams, apart from hospitals in Lancashire. When we played against the East Lancashire team there was a full day. Oh yeah.

Every Christmas we put on a pantomime. Staff put it on, female and male. You mention it we had it. Some wonderful singers: Steve Dulcamara, John Dixon, Bert Burrows.

Comedians: Harry Ward. Magicians. We used to put it on and take the Grand Theatre in town, or the town hall ... When I see such as Lily Savage or Danny La Rue... we had a character, a feller called David Wilson, he was marvellous. I can see him now. You'd see him during the daytime working, and then see him on the stage, you wouldn't believe it: he was beautiful. And we had artists. At Christmastime every ward used to have a scene of some description. The first one that I saw was at Christmas in '38. I was working in a ward called A Ward and they put on a scene of the Lambeth Way. It looked as though there was a hole dug in the floor, with things round and dummies and what have you. And Number One Ward had the Cresta Run. Oh there were some very, very good artists.

Every ward was locked, every member of the staff had a key plus a tap key. A tap key was so you could turn on the hot water, or get into the telephone which was in a box. Which was rather stupid when you think back. In those days on every ward (as I keep saying, I can only quote the male wards) coming out of the wall, down the corridor, there was naked flame – so that patients could have a smoke, light their own cigarettes. The floors was wooden tiles and, literally, they were very, very highly polished. Think about what a fire-risk that could be! Open fires in the wards. Well there was a so-called central heating but they had open fires. Remember this, in those days there was no domestic staff. Oh God, no! All the cleaning had to be done by the staff and patients. You see in those days, pre-war, the staffing on the ward was anything from twelve to fourteen on each ward and over a hundred patients. In '38 there'd be about 3,000 patients up there. But as I say, we had to do our own cleaning and what have you. We were hairdressers, chiropodists, shavers, cleaning windows, we had it all to do. We had our own fire brigade. Where the dispensary was, next to the enquiry office, well that used to be the fire station. Oh yeah, we had our own fire brigade. And that had to be with staff labour, you know. Because on each ward you had to have people sleeping on the ward; you had to live in the hospital when you first started. 'Cause you were on call, you see, in case something happened. It happened quite a lot. A heck of a lot [of staff] had to live in the hospital.

There used to be three categories of patients who were on parole; it took a long time to get though, 'cause everything was so strict. Patients used to go out for walks, sometimes just in the grounds with staff and sometimes they'd go up into the country, right round Quernmore. Some got parole for in the grounds only, then it went onto grounds and country, then it went into town but they were very, very few and far between. As I say, I'm talking pre-war here. Campbell House was known as the Gentlemens' Villa, for male private patients, and Ridge Lea was known as the Ladies' Villa and they were all female private patients.

Lancaster Moor Hospital was a community. They had their own farms, piggeries, bake-house, two churches. They had their own cinema, which was put on every week. They had their own coach to take patients for trips out. It was a community within itself. The farms, the gardens, the grounds, the piggeries, the boiler house, all this was done with patient and staff labour; this where your attendant come in. But everything was done. When I see today, these old people sitting in a ward right round doing nothing. To think back, we used to take patients out, they were mobile all the time. The patients knew what they were going to do. They were not forced, not: 'You are going to work on the land. You are going to work in the piggeries!' Nothing like that. Everybody seemed to have their own little niche in the place.

I was away for six years in the Far East during the war. Things altered after the war tremendously. When I came back here we had a medical superintendant called Dr Joseph Silverstone. He was far-seeing. He wanted to drag the hospital from the 1800s to the modern era and have good qualified staff… So then I qualified as a state-registered nurse and I also qualified as a registered mental nurse. Time goes on, and then I went to Salford Royal and I was taught neurosurgery. This was the progression. You see, pre-war if you'd have asked me what treatments there were, well it was literally, more-or-less non-existent. In the main, patients were given paraldehyde, which was liquid and they drank it. You could always tell, it stunk worse than people having garlic, and that's awful. Well it just kept them down, it was given at night-time as a seda-tive. If my memory serves me correctly, and I think I'm right, just after the war two drugs were brought in called triazol and cardiazol, which was injections which brought on epi-leptic seizures. And of course then the ECT came and the tranquilisers: the largactil and the other things. The pre-frontal leucotomy, I never rated it but… So with the advent of a lot of the tranquilisers, the aggressive patients, as we knew it then, gradually came down and down. In short, it certainly did a lot of good. The time came that gradually one ward was opened, then two, then they all were opened and everybody mixed. A lot of things hap-pened round about then, just after the war, because then you started having domestic staff coming in for cleaning the wards; you started having occupational therapists, chiropodists, hairdressers. We still did the shaving… Female nurses worked on the male wards which was unknown pre-war… I liked it far better post-war because you could see everything becoming more beneficial – for the staff, for the patients, for the community. So you could see an improvement all the way through.

Herbert Lowe (b. 1920)

Errand boy

When I was eleven years of age I got my first job as a baker's boy at the Empire Café in Market Street. The Empire Café was where that music shop, HMV, is now right opposite the fountain. I only worked there on Saturdays and I used to work from nine o'clock in a morning till six o'clock at night. And I can't quite remember which but I got either two shillings or two shillings and sixpence. And of course I got my lunch there and when I'd finished work at night they used to give me a bag of cakes to take home as well. During the day I used to have a basket over my arm and I used to take boxes of fancy cakes all over Lancaster. They made their order and I delivered it. You don't get much of that today. I used to go up Scotforth, over Skerton, all over.

Market Square from the museum steps in 1937, with the Empire Café visible between the pillars.

One of the errands that I used to really enjoy going to was Lancaster Castle. At that time the young police recruits were trained up at the castle. I used to have a wooden tray with loaves on it that were about two foot long and six inches square, so that they could put them in a slicing machine, and I used to balance the tray on my head, walk up to the castle, ring the bell and the warder used to come out and take me through to the kitchen. I used to stop in the yard at the castle watching them do their PT and unarmed combat. I'd be thirteen years of age the next job I got. I worked evenings and all day Saturday at Mr Dilworth's grocer shop in Aldcliffe Road. The shop is still there and still being used, it's in the square... I was paid four shillings and sixpence working after school till half past seven and all day Saturday. But the advantage for me was that there was a bicycle with a carrier on the front. I used to deliver groceries all over the Lancaster area... So really I was quite chuffed with being a wage earner. My mother used to say: 'Our Charlie he buys the Sunday dinner he does.'

Charlie Adams (b. 1917)

Factories

There used to be loads of factories in Lancaster. There was Lansil, there was Standfast, Storey's, Nelson's, Williamson's... Nisbett's on North Road, K Shoes. Oh there was slipper factories, there was two ... and Decorous Garments. There was Hornsea Pottery as well... If you didn't like the job you could just leave it and go and get another one straight away. I had my job before I left school. And I had a choice of going in the offices at Lansil or the factory, and I chose the factory because it was more money... I left school on the Friday, I was fourteen on the Saturday, and I started work on the Monday at Lansil in circular knitting. We used to make underwear. And I always remember, you know, that with being

A 1956 aerial view of the Lansil factory on Caton Road.

Greenfield Mill (c.1970), photographed shortly before it was demolished. The low, flat-roofed building at the front was originally one of the mill's three reservoirs but in 1940 it was drained and rebuilt as a large air-raid shelter for the workers.

just leaving school, when I wanted to go to toilet I used to put my hand up: 'Please Miss' to supervisor.

Audrey Entwistle, *née* Bleasdale (b. 1928)

Williamson's

I left school at the October break when I was fourteen. I left on a Friday and started work at Williamson's on the Monday. I only had the weekend off. It was during the war and I started work down near Carlisle Bridge, the 'Top Shop' they used to call it. You used to get big bundles of these fireproof gloves for the Army, and you used to just tie left and right hand gloves together. When the Top Shop shut down the next job I got was in the weighing office and then I started filling in on tables and doing patterns on lino. I had to leave for a bit, of course, while I had my family and after that I used to get odd jobs in the same place. I worked in the tile shop from six till ten until the kiddies got to school and then when my husband died I got a full-time job in the pattern room and I was there till I retired when I was sixty. I worked for Williamson's since I was fourteen really; there were just breaks where I had my children but they always took me back.

Peggy Phillips, *née* Thomas (b. 1926)

Engraver at Williamson's and Storey's

I started at the shipyard, Williamson's, in 1943 when I was fourteen. First of all I was in what they call edge minding in printers, then I went into the engravers as an apprentice. Fred Willoughby was an engraver there and he used to have classes for us young lads at night time and weekends at what was called the Lancaster Dinner Hour Club in what was known as the Top Shop – that was in the old St George's Works on the quay. It was used as the workplace for the war effort as well. I was

serving a seven year apprenticeship but when I was eighteen I went in the Army for two years national service. I went back to work after that to finish my apprenticeship and I didn't come out of my time till I was twenty-three. When I came out of my time I went to Storey's as an engraver and I worked at Storey's for forty-one years till I retired.

Ken Lambert (b. 1929)

The knocker-up

My grandad, Anthony Ginocchio, he worked at Williamson's in the shipyard. And when we first moved on Chestnut Grove in 1935, I don't think a lot of people had clocks then and they used to work shifts at the mills. He used to get up about four o'clock and he used to go out with a long wooden pole and tap on

Anthony Ginocchio, the Marsh Estate's knocker-up in the 1930s and '40s.

Women working in Williamson's Department 12X in the 1950s.

Workers leaving Williamson's Lune Mills site, better known as 'The Shipyard'.

Lord Peel visiting lads at the Dinner Hour Club in 1942.

windows. He was the knocker-up for them to go to work. I think he charged a penny a week.

Betty Cummings, *née* Hargreaves (b. 1927)

When Betty and Joan Hargreaves' grandad used to be the knocker-up on the Marsh, I remember him. He used to have a pole like a clothes prop and then he used to put a garden cane on the end taped on. He didn't knock on the door, he always knocked on the bedroom window and if you were just waking up it made you jump and you used to jump out of bed.

Ken Lambert (b. 1929)

Williamson's and Storey's had sirens outside but if you didn't get in to work before the sirens finished you were off for the day. They would shut the door. And if you didn't work you didn't get paid. People used to run down the street like hell because once the siren finished, that was it for the day, they'd lock the gates and you would not get in. That's why they had knockers-up, so that they'd get there in time. If you didn't work you didn't get paid.

Maureen Palwankar, *née* Schofield (b. 1942)

Waring and Gillows to the Royal Albert

I went to St Peter's School till I was fourteen and I went to work at Waring and Gillows on war work. I used to mix the glue for the aircraft frames. There was an old man, his name was Joe Taylor, and he was a master carver. He was a lovely man and he used to let you use his tools. Being a master carver, every one of his tools had a different carved handle. He used to let you use them but he says: 'First time you ever put 'em back in wrong shop!' Because his eyes never left what

he was doing, he'd just put his hands out and he knew which tool he had from its place. He was a wonderful old man. He showed me how to make galleons and things like that. I left Gillows and I went in the Royal Horse Artillery for three years' national service, in Palestine mainly. I went in just as the war finished. And then I came home and I went back to Gillows. They couldn't get French polishers and they were doing a lot of ships, liners, and they sent me on a shortened course (three years instead of five) on French polishing. But I couldn't settle because of the unions. The lads that had been to war were alright, they were no problem, but those that had had a sheltered life, they got nasty. So I went to work at the Royal Albert in 1957 and I was there thirty-one years. Enid, my wife, was there twenty-eight years. She was an SEN on nights and I was a charge nurse on days.

Ralph Wilson (b. 1927)

Hiring Fair on Cornmarket Street

Leaving school at fourteen I started work in the pattern department at Jas Williamson's. I was there for three years and then went to work for Seward's, heating engineers, in Market Street. But the late 1920s and early '30s were really depressed years and after two years I was made redundant. Business wasn't so hot. After I'd been there two years, I had to be made redundant. Things weren't going so well anywhere in the country, they were laying single fellers off and keeping married men, that was the ticket. There was so much unemployment. I remember seeing a queue of fellers all the way along King Street waiting to sign on at the labour exchange which was where the assembly rooms are now. There were so many of them, you'd think they were going into a football match. Right across the road from there, before the market was altered, it was Cornmarket Street, where the old Coffee Tavern was, outside the rear of the market entrance. And that's where they did all the hiring for farm lads at certain times of the year, before the harvest; that's where they used to take them on for twelve months or six months or whatever. They used to smack their hands as soon as they made a bargain. In fact the Irish lads used to come over and a lot of them used to get jobs. The name for them was the July barbers because they used to come over every summer; they'd come off farms and they were used to agriculture … the farmers used to be there and they used to make a deal with each other: so much a quarter or something like that. I was only a boy then but I used to hang around listening to them, you know… The Coffee Tavern was in the corner of Cornmarket Street and you could smell the coffee there, and the big meat pies, and all us kids used to be looking at these guys.

Charlie Adams (b. 1917)

Buck Ruxton's children

In 1935 I was working as a children's nurse at Parkside Children's Home. Parkside was next to the workhouse on Quernmore Road in a separate building for the children. Ruxton's three children finished up there but they didn't mix with the other children. They were looked after and taught by the matron and the master in the main building. Mr and Mrs Tomlinson were the master and matron at that time. It was a secret in Lancaster, nobody knew where they had gone. I only found out that they were there by accident. I saw a slipper with the name Elizabeth sewn into it and was told by my sister, who was a more senior nurse, to keep quiet. The children: Diane, Elizabeth and little Billy, were there about two or three years and then when they got older they sent them away. We never knew where they went, the matron would have known but not even my sister was told.

Civic dignitaries visiting Parkside Children's Home at Christmas time in the late 1930s. Mary Tolson is the young nurse wearing a white cap in the centre.

I knew the children before all the scandal when Dr Buck Ruxton murdered their mother and Mary Rogerson. The children's nurse, Mary Rogerson, used to walk them round the streets and she used to call in to my mum's house on the top end of King Street to take them to the toilet. I can remember them; they were nice-mannered and Mary Rogerson was lovely, very polite. Dr Ruxton was a very good family doctor. His wife, she liked the men. She used to go up to Quernmore with this chap from the town hall. People used to see them there.

Mary Hodgson, *née* Tolson (b. 1918)

The Depression

I was born in 1928 on Alexander Road, Skerton: a 'Wapping Lad'. They called Skerton 'Wapping', I don't know why. It was a two-up and two-down. My parents were Jack and Beatrice and I had two sisters, Ivy and Jessie, and a brother Reg that's twelve years older than me. We lived in a two-up, two-down with outside toilet, tin bath. I don't know how the hell we lived in it really, when you think there was four kids and two grown-ups. And then it was coming up to the Depression. Me father worked for Waring and Gillows and they were always in and out of work. He says, 'I'll get a job' and he walked from Lancaster to Leyland and he managed to get a job up at Leyland Motors.

Jack Watson (b. 1928)

Varey's Scrapyard is now an underground car park

I was born Joan Woodend on Westham Street in 1931. I married my husband Daniel Varey in 1950. My sister Eileen and I married two brothers, she married David Varey.

The Varey's lived over Skerton and they must have been a travelling family because they go up to Appleby every June. I have a photograph taken in about 1936 of travellers from Skerton up at Appleby. There's Dick Sowerby in it and my husband Daniel Varey,

Travellers (including the Varey and Sowerby families) from Skerton at Appleby Horse Fair, *c.* 1936.

Jackie Lambert, Thomas Varey and David Varey on the Pinfold Lane site before Varey's Garage was built.

Varey's scrapped cars are now buried under King George's Playing Fields.

when they were little boys, and Nina Varey, and Mrs Varey, Dan's mother, and Dorothy Varey, Uncle Dave's wife, and Shirley Varey when she was a baby. The Varey's had two scrapyards and a lot of property. The scrapyards were on the back of Vale Road and they had the dairy on Central Avenue and the garages on Pinfold Lane. The grandma and the grandad lived at the top of Pinfold Lane. It's a right old house if you see it. It was two cottages at one time. The granny, they called her Jemima Gentle, she had these two cottages made into one. And he used to go up every day, did Mr Varey, to see she was okay. Mr Varey was Thomas Varey, David and Daniel's father.

Where Varey's garage was, there's eight houses built there now. If you go down Pinfold Lane, there's eight houses there now. The scrapyard at the back of Vale Road used to be full of cars. And Mr Varey got these cars off Barton Townley, he used to buy them off him. You know, if people bought new ones, Mr Varey used to buy the trade-ins off him. And they're actually still in that quarry and they've filled it in. The corporation made a compulsory purchase of the land in 1966 but they didn't clear the cars, there's hundreds of them all still underneath the ground. It's just filled in. It's just ground.

Joan Varey, *née* Woodend (b. 1931)

On 28 February 1966 a 250ft works chimney weighing 3,300 tons suddenly collapsed at Storey's White Cross factory. This photograph was taken in the immediate aftermath of the disaster.

five

Leisure

Chasing lasses and 'The Walk'

After leaving school, we started chasing lasses then. On a Saturday night we used to go to Green Ayre Station and for ten pence they used to give us a four penny return ticket to Promenade Station and a six penny ticket into the Winter Gardens. For that you saw the show till half past ten and then got into the ballroom. We used to go dancing till about twenty past eleven and dash for the last train then. For ten pence you had a good night out! We used to get some good dances in the Phoenix Hall as well, where the Territorial Army used to train.

Sunday night was spent by young lads and lasses walking round 'The Walk' as they called it: King Street, Common Garden Street, Penny Street and Market Street. We used to walk round there meeting each other. Then we used to go into Frances Passage to the milk bar and get a milkshake. You used to go dancing on a Saturday night and then you used to go on 'The Walk' on a Sunday, meeting different ones and making arrangements to go dancing next Saturday night. It was a meeting place for everybody. You'd get two or three lasses together and two or three lads together, walking round, then you'd stop and have a talk and then say cheerio and go off a bit further.

We went to the pictures as well. I used to go mostly to the Picturedrome, Palladium, County and Palace; I never used to go to the Odeon so much but I used to go to the others regularly. The County and the Picturedrome were two of the favourites.

Bill Stockdale (b. 1923)

'That's all there was in them days, dancing and cinemas'

As a teenager, at weekends I used to go mostly to the Alex, as the Alexandra Hotel used to be called, at the top of Penny Street. We used to go dancing there in the wartime; the army were stationed at St Thomas's, where Ripley School is now, and that used to be the place where they went. That's all there was in them days: dancing and cinemas. We had lots of cinemas here in Lancaster. There was the Kingsway on Parliament Street. When we lived over Skerton I used to take our Doreen over Skerton Bridge to the Saturday morning pictures there and we always used to sing things. In Dalton Square there was the Palace and, next to Dr Buck Ruxton's, the County. And then there was what we used to call the 'Bug Hut' – that was the Picturedrome. We used to say 'Go in and laugh, come out and scrat.' They used to have these 'love seats' upstairs, they didn't have an arm between them and they were up in the balcony for couples. The Bug Hut used to be at the bottom of Church Street, across where the car park is and the Sally's Army, as we used to call it, was next door to it. And then there was the Odeon, which is still there, and there was one in Market Street, the Palladium, where W.H. Smith is now.

Peggy Phillips, *née* Thomas (b. 1926)

The picture houses

When I was a young lad living on Skerton we used to go to the Kingsway on Parliament Street. We saw lots of pictures, mainly cowboys such as Roy Rodgers and also the Three Stooges, Charlie Chaplin and Charlie Chan. They had competitions on the stage like card games and apple dipping from a tub, which was a big treat in those days. Sometimes me and my mates, we didn't have enough money to all pay to go in to see the film, so two would pay at the door and then go to the boys toilets and let the other two in through the back door. Or sometimes we'd sneak in through the fire door. Times were hard then so we'd do jobs for people to get money to go to the pictures. We'd take empty bottles back to the shop and collect the deposits, or we'd go to the

Dancers at the masked ball held in the Ashton Hall on New Year's Eve, 1928.

Orchestra and helpers at the masked ball held on New Year's Eve 1928 in the Ashton Hall.

The County Cinema, Dalton Square, 1937. In 1935, in the house next door, Dr Buck Ruxton murdered his common-law wife Isabella and their maid, Mary Rogerson. He was hanged in Strangeways Prison in 1936.

coal yard at Green Ayre, get a bag of coal in a buggy and then push it all the way home, just for coppers. Or we'd go to the tip and pick coke for the fire. We only went to The Grand a few times, it was too posh inside for us lads.

We liked the Bug Hut more. That was the Picturedrome on Lower Church Street – also known as the 'Bug Hut' or the 'Laugh 'n' Scrat'. The queues for that started at Horse Shoe Corner and went right down Lower Church Street to the Sally Army Hut. We always watched the band marching and playing and then going into their hut, everybody gave them a good cheer. The Picturedrome was always full and going there was a real novelty to us. I remember once a crowd of people protesting because Sunday was a religious day but it was always very popular. You had to get there early to get a decent seat or you ended up on the Monkey Rack

right at the back, or even worse you could sit on the pipes going round the inside. But you had to fold you coat up underneath you to sit on because the pipes were so hot they made you sweat like a pig. There used to be a shop right across from the Bug Hut in Lower Church Street called Woods's Pet Shop. And we used to buy parched peas from there to eat in pictures, or we used to throw them about as well. It sounds funny, getting parched peas from a pet shop but they were maple peas that they feed pigeons with. We used to buy tame white mice from Woods's as well and we used to put 'em on lasses' seats in pictures and say 'Hey, there's a mouse!' and they'd jump. A Mr Ackroyd, or Holroyd, would come round with his torch and if anyone made a noise you got thrown out by the man with one arm.

The Palace, in Dalton Square, was where the organ rose up to the stage level and always played before the picture started. I remember seeing the film *Gone With The Wind* – it was the first time we had an interval in the big film because it was a really long film. When the war started we used to see Winston Churchill giving his speeches to the troops and special news programmes. And after the war we saw pictures of the terrible concentration camps. People in the cinema were crying and leaving their seats because they couldn't watch any more, it brought back so many memories. I only started going to the County when I started courting, just before I started my call-up in the Army. It was next to Buck Ruxton's house in Dalton Square. There were always long queues right down Great John Street. The Palladium was next door to Bate and Gorst Chemist in Market Square. It wasn't a very big place though and I didn't like it. The Odeon on King Street was the posh one. I went there on Saturday mornings as a boy, then after the war I went there quite a lot. They always had the best films and nice seats that folded up and down. There were lots of refreshments too but also long queues.

Ken Lambert (b. 1929)

I had a grandma, Emily Purchase, who used to be the midwife at Caton, and she came to live with us for a time when she got older. She lived between all her daughters and there was a family of thirteen of them. So she used to come and stay with us for six months and then she'd move on to the next one for six months; this is how they used to look after the old, not put them in a home like they do now. She used to take me down to the Picturedrome. I can always remember, the film at the Picturedrome changed every two days. The Picturedrome was known as the 'Bug Hut' down at the bottom of Church Street. It was right at the bottom of Church Street on the right-hand side. The Salvation Army was

next to it, right opposite the White Horse, that's called Paddy Mulligan's now. She was well known and we used to get in for nothing because the bloke on the door knew us. He used to say 'Oh come in, you're alright.'

I can always remember going along Church Street afterwards slapping my backside thinking I was Hopalong Cassidy. We used to go down there a couple of times a week. We used to go and see films like *Gunga Din* and serials like *Flash Gordon* every week.

Jack Watson (b. 1928)

Dance bands and amateur dramatics

I've always sung. I used to sing going down the middle of the road in the blackout because I was frightened of the dark! The first band I sang with was 'Tony Troughton and his Hawaiian Serenaders'. There used to be a girl in that called Joan Radcliffe, and there was Jackie Renshaw, and the other lad was Ronnie Devanney. Now he used to sing with a group at the time called Stefani's Silver Songsters. He lived on Blades Street. And that's when I first started singing. You might remember the shops Kenneth Gardner's Electrics? Well Kenneth Gardner was the dad and he was a fire officer and he used to run a big band. Periodically, they'd call on me and ask if I'd come and do a song. And because we were hard up he'd always give my mam a couple of bob.

And I played drums. I used to have two metal files in my pocket when I worked at Waring and Gillows and I used to drive 'em mad drumming with these files. I used to wear the fences away. My mum could never afford any drums and there was a bloke at Waring and Gillows and he always said 'If I ever win them coupons, I'll buy you some drums!' And he did: he won £30,000 and this was during the war. But he never bought me any drums. When I was in the army I got a telephone call from a lieutenant saying 'I believe you play the

June Hampshire and the Sunshine Follies in 1943, including fourteen year old Olive Bainbridge. They were a tap-dancing troupe of girls from Skerton School who provided entertainment at various venues during wartime.

drums.' Well I'd never played drums in my life; I'd wanted to but I'd never played a drum. He sent a jeep for me and I had to have a go on the drums and I finished up playing with the Army band. I also used to sing. We broadcast home on a Tuesday night, for half an hour on British Forces Radio. The top of the hit parade then was 'Nancy With the Laughing Face' and for about eight weeks I had to sing it because they called one of the blokes' wives Nancy.

And then I came home and joined a lady called Mary Beamer's band. She played piano and I had quite a few years playing the drums and singing with her. We played at Lansil Club and loads of other places. She was a lovely person. I also played for Mollie Cowan's kids dancing school concerts over the years. Then I went playing in clubs. I had three spells with Harold Graham the organist. He taught me a lot did Harold, just by playing with him. We played at Morecambe Football Club for about eight years.

Meanwhile, I was involved in the Red Rose: Lancaster Red Rose Amateur Dramatics and Operatic Society. I joined them in 1941 when I was fourteen. I started off in the concert party. The war was still on and you went all over, entertaining in village halls to keep people happy. I met Enid, my wife, at the Red Rose. I did my first show, *No, No Nanette*, in the town hall when I was sixteen. I was in the chorus for many years. Then I played small parts and my first big lead was when I was forty-one, in *Half a Sixpence*.

Theatre was really popular when I first started. We used to queue up all Sunday night to book tickets on the Monday morning in Cornthwaite's sweet shop in Dalton Square, that was used as the Red Rose booking office. It's not there now. It was just next to the Palace, that's Brook's nightclub now. And the earliest I ever went was two o'clock on a Sunday afternoon, to buy front seat tickets at nine o'clock the following Monday morning. Now this is true. The police station used to be

CHITTERLOW
Les Kenyon

KIPPS
Ralph Wilson

Kipps : "Arthur Kipps—that's me."

Ralph Wilson and Les Kenyon starring in *Half A Sixpence* at the Grand Theatre in 1968.

Mollie Cowan, the dancing mistress for many years, who was succeeded by her daughter. Mollie's son, Michael Dowthwaite, got his fifty year medal last year and he's still performing. It was a family do in the old days. We have Kathleen, myself and Margery Bargh who are the recipients of a diamond bar for sixty years service. Jean Dent, *née* Kirkbride, she's got her fifty year medal. A lot of people have been in it a long time. I've never been in any other society. We always class it as 'The Friendly Society' because we've all been friends for so many years and we're still there. I've enjoyed it and they've been good times. I love singing and dancing and drumming. I'm just musical. I've never had a lesson in my life and to this day I can't read a note. I've always sung and played by ear. I love being in the Red Rose and that's it. It's been my life for sixty-four years. I found my wife and made life-long friends there.

Ralph Wilson (b. 1927)

down the side of the town hall then and we were stood outside the door and I can still see this bobby now: he came out and he said 'You want locking up you do, you want putting in that hospital up there', which was the Moor Hospital. It would probably get to about three in the morning and then she'd open the shop and let you in but you couldn't buy the tickets till nine o'clock. The men used to play cards in the shop to pass the time. Then their wives would come about 8 o'clock and take over and they would go to work.

We've had friends in the Red Rose for yonks. Kathleen Kenyon, our producer, used to play parts and she's been producing since the early fifties. She met her husband, Les Kenyon, there. Les played comedy leads for years. Oh he was funny. Kathleen's worked hard for years: it's an unpaid position and she's a true amateur. Her mother, Bertha, was a founder member in 1935 and so I think was

Dance halls

In Morecambe there was the Foral, Pier, Winter Gardens and Tower and in Lancaster it was the Alex. And sometimes they had special ones at the Phoenix. And the Jubilee Hall on China Street, they used to have dances in there…We used to go into Morecambe every Saturday. I went to the Floral. Sometimes we used to go to Floral two or three times a week and it was always Friday and Saturday dancing, and then Sunday the pictures… The last train was eleven o'clock. Then I had to walk home on Morecambe Road, you know. But you felt safe them days… I used to work at Lansil; this was before I was married. I worked at Lansil and I used to go to work early in the morning, you know, before we started at a quarter to eight. And if we were going to Floral that night, we always took our curlers and put our turban on, you know. Then we used to go to

The Winter Gardens in Morecambe, c.1935.

Floral at night and go in dressing room and take 'em out.

Audrey Entwistle, *née* Bleasdale (b. 1928)

The Tower Ballroom had the best dance floor in Morecambe

We always went dancing at the Tower when we were younger. The best floor in Morecambe was the Tower, sprung floor, it was smashing. I remember, it was one of my mates' twenty-first and I went down with her. And she got a bit tipsy and she said 'You see that gang of lads down there, come down with me cos I'm gonna ask one of them for a dance.' So I went down with her and she said 'I'm twenty-one today can I have this dance?' And he said 'No, you can dance with my mate, I'm taking your mate on.' That's when I started going out with my husband. I met my husband, John Snape, at the Tower Ballroom at Morecambe. He said he

could always remember me as a little girl, when I lived on South Edward Street, sat on doorstep selling periwinkles at a penny a cup. My grandad used to go and collect 'em and he used to boil 'em and then I had the job of selling 'em. I must have sold them all in about three quarters of an hour. Everybody used to come with cups and have a cup of periwinkles. He said 'I can remember you, a snotty-nosed little kid with bright ginger hair selling periwinkles.' I had really carroty hair when I was young.

Marlene Snape, *née* Campbell (b. 1932)

Pub life

We moved into the Black Bull on China Street in 1938, when I was ten. It's now called the Duke of Lancaster. My parents were Jack and Beatrice and I had two sisters, Ivy and Jessie, and a brother Reg. I was the youngest. My grandma and her husband had a flat in the

The Castle Hotel on China Street. The man outside is possibly Walter Rainbird, who Charlie Adams (who owns the photo) remembers as being the manager.

An early photograph of the Park Hotel receiving a delivery of beer in around 1900.

The Spinners Arms, which was on Aldcliffe Road.

The Carpenter's Arms at the bottom of Bridge Lane, now named the Three Mariners.

top of the pub and my auntie used to work in the bar. I also had another grandma, Emily Purchase, who used to be the midwife at Caton, and she came to live with us for a time when she got old.

You had the vaults where all the men drank, then you had a snug where the women drank, then you had a smoke room where you could go in and smoke, and then you had a commercial room which was a bit classy: they were the posh lot in there. You didn't smoke in the commercial room that was all but you smoked in the smoke room. You always got toffee-nosed people that didn't like the smokers. The snug was more-or-less for women and anybody who wanted to come in and take beer out. They used to come in with a jug and ask for a couple of pints of beer put in it.

We used to have a lot of celebrities coming in: we had Tucker Smith, who was a champion boxer, and Billy Hodgon. My dad liked being in the vaults, he liked to talk to the fighters. We even had all-in-wrestlers from the Winter

Gardens at Morecambe. My sister used to take me down to watch them. They used to fight like hell and then at ten o'clock at night who comes in the pub but two of the wrestlers, Cocky Knight and Jack Pye. They'd come walking in the pub and stand against the bar and my sister used to say 'We've just been down and you were tearing one another to pieces!' And they used to say 'Well it was only a bit of fun.'

On China Street during the war, there was the Jubilee Hall where they used to have theatre acts like comedians and singers and they used to have these dog turns. The dog bloke, John Watson, would stay with us and we used to have about twenty dogs in the garage at the pub and him stopping upstairs.

The Black Bull was very busy with all the lodging houses around. We had an average of about fifty customers in the pub every night, regulars they never missed, and twenty five or thirty during the dinnertime. They used to come in for their lunch, have a pint, go back to work, come in again at half-past five, go home for their tea and then come back again at about seven o'clock. This is how the men lived in those days because the wife was at home and they thought if they earned the money they'd leave the poor wives at home. And they used to play dominoes and cards and things like this. Most of them worked at Williamson's or Storey's and I've seen the women on a Friday night actually waiting outside for them before they went in the pub, to get their money off them so they didn't gamble it away on the tables. I remember one night, a woman coming in the pub, with a black eye. And my mother says 'What's wrong with you?' And she says 'Wait while he comes round!' And her husband had his head all bandaged. She'd hit him over the head with the rolling pin.

They used to have big fights in them places, you know. Oh aye, especially in the Black Bull. I can always remember in the Black Bull one night, hearing a scuffle and going in, and my auntie hit one of the blokes over the head with a bottle and they dragged a little bloke called Barney Golding, who was a referee in the North Lancashire League, over the counter with his tie and they were trying to cut his tie off before it choked him, you know. It was a real rough house.

At the end of 1943 we went to the Park Hotel up Primrose. We had another good vault up there again because we had the Army barracks there. And I can always remember my mother used to say 'I could do with some more tea' and she used to tap the army lads up 'Can you get me more tea?' A truck would come down with all these tea chests on full of tea and they said 'Here you are love.' We only needed one of them and it lasted us till end of war! But we used to have to give them a bit back.

And I even remember it was rationed was beer, so we could only get so much a time. I can even remember them asking for the dregs, you know the dregs that go over the side of the glass, and filling glasses up so they could have another drink. We didn't have to have coupons for beer but we had coupons for clothes, food, things like that. It was lovely. It's a lot different now. We used to have a really good snug in the Park, which was like a jug and bottle. We had one in the Black Bull as well. I'd never met characters like them. They used to come in and they used to drink Guinness and Worthingtons. They used to get as drunk as hell and then I used to get serenaded all night by these three old ladies. It was lovely.

Jack Watson (b. 1928)

The Victoria Hotel snug

I remember the snug in the Vic. You went in through door and there was like a corridor. You went down corridor and the snug was on corner there. 'Cause if you, by accident, opened that door you used to get blasted out. It was same crowd that went in every night, you know, it was their place and that was it… They went every night and that was it. And it was the same people that sat in the same seats. It was only a right small room but they used to have fire blazing, you know coal on, and they used to hit it with a bottle to break coal… Old Mrs Bateson and her son used to go in. There'd be about twenty or so, all drinking bottles.

Maureen Palwankar, *née* Schofield (b. 1942)

In the Vic there used to be about half a dozen old ladies used to go in that 'little snug room' as they called it. They all had their own seats. I can remember that, and nobody dared sit on their seat… And I can remember when the Guinness, it used to be cold… They wouldn't drink it cold… He [the landlord] used to leave it in the snug for the day to make it warm enough for them to drink.

Gloria Dunstan, *née* Dunne (b. 1946)

The Lads Club

As a youngster I used to attend a small boys club run by the TOCH and it was situated in China Street above where the pet shop is now. A group of men used to run it for us and there used to be boxing, games, etcetera. The chap I remember most of all was a Mr Woods who was a local businessman. I believe he was a tailor. He had premises in Sir Simon's Arcade. And he used to be the chief committee member, he used to look after it. But when the Lancaster Lads Club opened that was the best thing that ever happened to the youth of Lancaster. There was every facility there: all sorts of athletics and exercises and games to play, reading places, keep-fit classes, everything that a young lad would appreciate. The chap that used to keep us in order was a retired fireman by the name of Mr Vickers. The first lads club that opened, it was a long black hut in Dallas Road. One of the big supporters was a man by the name of Mr Penney and he lived nearby on Dallas Road and he used to support us financially and physically. I went to the lads club right from the start of it opening in about 1929/30.

Charlie Adams (b. 1917)

I remember the first time I saw the boys club. There was a night game at the Giant Axe; it was still Lancaster Town then, it wasn't a city

Terry Deehan during one of Jimmy Downham's football coaching sessions at the Lads Club on Dallas Road, c.1970.

Jimmy Downham outside the Lads Club.

till 1937. Me and my brothers went down to the game while there was still light. There were no floodlights, worst thing ever invented floodlights! And we came back down Dallas Road and the boys club. It was a long hut which had been used for horses during the First World War. This was 1932, I was twelve nearly thirteen. And we looked inside this club and do you know what first struck me about it? The warmth, the heat coming out of it. And at thirteen, my two brothers and myself, we joined. And we didn't have a penny to join but they said that's alright, come in. It was a fantastic club. It was packed and packed because there was a need of it then. In 1937 they built the present building and whilst I was in and out of the old club I saw every brick and floorboard of the new club laid.

Jimmy Downham (b. 1920)

Teddy boys and girls

I was a Teddy girl: white ankle socks, red skirt, hair in a pony tail, a good rock and roller. All the lads wi' Teddy boy jackets on… Macari's on North Road was where Teddy boys and Teddy girls hung out. That's where we used to meet and have one hot Vimto in winter and cold Vimto in summer. And have records on all night; just records, like a youth club really… I once bumped my head on jukebox, a lad had pulled chair away and I bumped my head, and record that came on was 'Hard Headed Woman!' I liked Elvis… We used to go to Fenton Street, trades hall, rock and rolling two nights a week. It was really good there.

Freda Simpson, *née* Banton (b. 1943)

Freeman's Wood was our Morecambe

Oh yeah, when we used to go down. Yes, that was our Morecambe, 'cause we couldn't afford anything else. And we used to go down and you know the Golden Ball? Well you could

Jean Gardner in the 1940s.

go across water there, you know, when tide was down, it wasn't deep. Men used to go and fetch bottles o' pop and beer for themselves and come back and we used to go treading flukes. Yeah, but I could never catch 'em. They used to tickle under me feet but I daren't pick 'em up… Oh they were funny. But we used to hold each others hand, you know, and go across that way. But we used to have some fun on Lune 'cause it wasn't like it is now, there was quite a bit o' sand that you could play on. Yeah. It wasn't like Morecambe or Blackpool sand but you could play on it… We always had picnics down there and kiddies used to all come down, any that their mothers wasn't going, they used to trail along wi' us, fetch their jam sandwiches or whatever their mother would put 'em up, aye and a bottle o' water.

Jean Brotheridge, *née* Gardner (b. 1925)

I had some friends on Denmark Street and some friends on Gerrard Street. We used to go out together... My auntie and uncle that lived on Wharfedale and we used to go down [to Freeman's Wood] as a family. There'd be eighteen or twenty. I remember, my uncle used to work for Alfred Street Laundry, Whiteside's... Occasionally he could have the van, so that would be a nice collection of family. And then we'd set off and we'd walk right through Freeman's Wood. They would take a tent. That was for changing, I guess. And we'd stay there all day. And it was lovely. And we'd do that regular... And because there's lots of currents in the river, it was very dangerous really, but they were good swimmers and they knew how to handle it. And my Uncle Jack used to swim me out because I was one of the smaller ones and so I couldn't be left. And there was great big cricket matches, rounders matches. It was wonderful.

Marlene Russell, *née* Ellwood (b. 1933)

We used to play jumping over the gulleys as well. Some of them were deep enough for kids to swim in... Me mam and our Ann, Annie Reed and that, we used to go down with the tent. Yeah!

Val Atkinson, *née* Clement (b. 1948)

The Easter Field

We used to go on the Easter Field first thing on Easter Monday morning and play football. Sometimes you got knocked out and then we used to roll eggs and do running. We used to have races, all organised, it was a smashing day out. I won a winners medal in 1934 playing for Marsh School.

Bill Stockdale (b. 1923)

And we used to play football on the Easter Field. All the schools used to play and we got a couple of medals playing for Greaves School there. Nowadays they still have the Easter Field but they don't have it like they used to. We used to roll the eggs and all that.

Jack Watson (b. 1928)

At Easter we used to get a ticket and we had to go to school Monday morning, Easter Monday morning, and there were these trestles and they were, oh there was all kinds of balls and books and cricket bats and stumps, tennis rackets. There was everything for a child. You got one of them free.

Jean Brotheridge, *née* Gardner (b. 1925)

Members of the Preston family sailing on the River Lune.

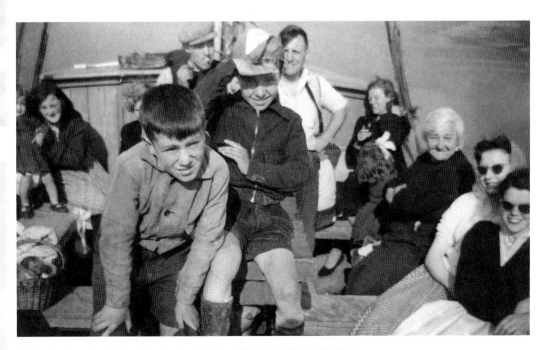

Above: Another generation of the Preston family and friends sailing on the Lune

Opposite above: Cathedral Primary School teams competing in the 1995 Easter Field competition.

Opposite below: Marsh Primary School, winners of the tournament on the Easter Field in 1997.

Six

Sport

Football crazy

Football's been my life; that is my story, from being a kid I loved it. I don't know where my interest came from because it wasn't in the family. Nobody taught me football, I learned it all myself, I was football daft. Right from when I played with a pig's bladder on the slates outside our house on Boundary Road. I would leave home on Saturday mornings, whatever the weather, and I would go and find football. I would walk to Barton Road and I would have galoshes on in the winter. We got cold winters then and it was really freezing. And I'd stand on Barton Road to watch the senior school, Greaves School. Now I was at Bowerham School then. My parents wouldn't

Jimmy Downham during his Second World War service as a machine gunner.

know where I was but you were quite safe in those days. If you got lost somebody would bring you home. And three or four times in the season I got a game when somebody didn't turn up. The master, Mr Jameson, would say 'Would you like to play?' Oh yes! And I'd run up and down this line with galoshes on. No football boots. I didn't have any football boots till I left school.

As well as football, the lads club is the most important part of my life really. I've played for several football teams over the years including professional stints for Lancaster City and Netherfield (although I never wanted to be paid for playing football – I would have paid to play!) but the team I was always happiest in was the Lads Club Old Boys. I joined them first when I was eighteen and we played on Aldcliffe Road. When I was twenty the war broke out and right through the war I had only one aim: watch after watch, I'd think of home and friends but I always just wanted to get back to the lads club and put back into it what I'd got out of it. And fortunately I did: I just retired last year after more than seventy years with the club, man and boy.

When the war broke out I wanted to join the Navy but everybody said 'Jim you're so left-handed, you'll be no good with knots' so I joined the Army. Then they wanted volunteers to go aboard merchant ships as machine-gunners. Well that suited me great. I was on different ships going round the Indian Ocean and at each port we would pull into we would take on water and fuel and it would take about four hours. In that time I would nip ashore. On every ship I had a football team and in any port we pulled in I'd organise a match.

I was eventually taken off ships and stationed in Bombay where football was promoted in a big way and I was in my element. Right opposite the naval barracks was the Cooperage, the Wembley Stadium of Bombay, and there was a game every night to entertain the troops

Above: Jimmy Downham leads out the Maritime Regiment to play against the Royal Navy XI in Bombay in 1945.

Above left: A surprise presentation to Jimmy Downham on completing forty years of service to Lancaster Boys Club in 1974. He then went on to serve the club for another thirty years!

Marsh Hornets AFC 1926/27.

Marsh boys' football teams outside St George's Church, Willow Lane, 1972.

Brookholme Rangers AFC
1923/24.

Skerton Athletic FC 1924/25.

Lancaster cricket team, c. 1982.

that were stationed there. I was beginning to be getting a name for football in India and in my time there I was welfare sergeant, arranging fixtures, and I not only captained my own Army side, the Maritime Regiment, but I captained the Royal Navy as well. I thought that was fantastic. How lucky! I was football stupid. But I've no regrets about being stupid. I got on very well with the professional players: England and Arsenal's number one right wing was in the RAF and we played in the same game. Then there was Langton, who played for Blackburn Rovers, they moved him inside to let me play left wing.

It was also in Bombay that I had the privilege of coming face to face with my boyhood hero. We couldn't afford a newspaper back on Boundary Road but there was always someone on the street who could and it was handed down. I remember this day, sat on the doorstep reading this newspaper, and I read about this gentleman footballer from Scotland. He was such a fantastic fellow. He played for Hearts. I would read about this man and I thought he must be a smashing bloke; Tommy Walker they called him. I sat on that doorstep at the Pointer, I think I'd be about ten or eleven, and read about this wonderful footballer.

And then along comes the war and I'm in India and talking to some Scottish RAF lads, telling them the story of how I'd read about this wonderful man, and one day they said 'Jimmy, do you want some good news?' They said 'Your pal will be here tomorrow, Tommy Walker.' He was in the RAF and they kept their good footballers back to entertain the troops. I gave him four or five days to settle and then we had a football match with my Army team. All I wanted was for these lads to have the privilege to say 'I played with Tommy Walker.' He was a gentleman, fantastic.

Fate has been good to me in many ways. On the day I retired as a painter and decorator at the Royal Albert, at the age of sixty-two, I was asked to coach the Marsh School football team and I carried that on for the next twenty-two years. Between that and the lads club, I've passed on my love of football to hundreds of boys and, in later years, girls too and made many friends but I've been the privileged one. I've been very, very fortunate in my life of football.

Jimmy Downham (b. 1920)

Anyone for tennis?

I was born, the only child of Horace and Nettie Riley, on West Road in 1928 and shortly afterwards went to live on Sibsey Street. I went to Dallas Road School until I was eight and then to the Friends School, the Quaker school which is no longer there now. I was ten when I started playing tennis on the Giant Axe field. There used to be grass courts there on the side of the football pitch. We moved to Hala Grove in 1938 and I joined Bowerham Tennis Club. I started to realise I was getting quite good at tennis. During the war the front part of the pavilion was taken over by the Home Guard and we had just the back of it. There was nothing else to do in wartime so we played tennis morning, afternoon and night in the holidays. When the war finished in 1945 I entered some tournaments and I was made captain of the Junior Lawn Tennis Club of Great Britain. I was only beaten twice in two years and I got to the last eight at Junior Wimbledon when I was seventeen. In 1947 I was called up and I went in the RAF to Germany. I won the RAF tennis championship both years I was in Germany and represented them in competitions. Coming out of the RAF, I would have liked to have had a year or two playing tennis but in those days it was very much amateur tennis so there was no money available at all. I had to work, and I worked for my father and uncle for about twenty years until my father retired.

In the meantime, I took the professional coaching course at Lilleshall under Dan Maskell. He was very interesting because he'd met all the world's best tennis players when he commentated at Wimbledon. So when I was thirty-four I became a professional tennis coach. I coached all over: Rossall School, Stoneyhurst College, Gleneagles, locally. And I worked for the Green Shield Stamp organisation which sponsored lots of coaching. I keep meeting people who say 'I was coached tennis by you.' Although I had to work (I owned and ran sports shops) I spent my holidays playing tennis and I won many senior LTA tournaments, both singles and doubles. I won the open mixed doubles tournament at Regent Park, Morecambe with Jean Mathews, daughter of Stanley Mathews. I also coached young Stanley Mathews, who was a keen tennis player, when his father was playing for Blackpool.

I retired at sixty and played more tennis and got a good group going at Lune Road Tennis Club. We played there every Tuesday and Thursday. I played veterans tennis for Lancashire. In my last game of competitive tennis I won the open mixed doubles with Michelle Noden at Lunesdale Lawn Tennis Club, Caton when I was sixty-four. That was my last game of competitive tennis because I had a heart attack after that and was advised not to play competitively.

I also started playing badminton in my twenties. We used to have a Lancaster and district tournament at the pier in Morecambe. It was extremely popular. We had mats down on the dance floor and we used to fill it. I got myself a good partner called Chris Thompson and we had a successful ten years together, when I was in my thirties and forties. We won the men's doubles several times. I finished my badminton career in my fifties at Hest Bank.

I've also always played table tennis. I was lucky because the headmaster of Friends School, 'Bulldog' Drummond, was keen on sport and he encouraged me. I managed to win the school tournament when I was twelve against some of the boys who were seventeen. I won the Lancaster Table Tennis Tournament on many occasions. I remember the many finals I had, mainly against Maurice Capstick and Ron Simmons. I left table tennis to play badminton and when I finished my badminton career I went back to it. I won the Kendal Open in my late fifties.

I still play table tennis: I won a tournament in Tenerife at the age of seventy-six and I've started playing locally at Ripley School where it's lovely to see so many young ones playing. I was also a member of Lancaster Golf Club for over fifty years. I played my golf mainly in winter because it fell in with the tennis. I had the pleasure of playing with Ian Hayes in the local Pro-Am for two years. He needed me mainly because of my handicap. I only finished playing golf two years ago and I'm still a social member of the club.

I met my first wife Sallie Little, whose family had Little's Jewellers on Church Street, when we were junior members of Bowerham Tennis Club. She had MS for forty years and we very much appreciated the support we got from the MS Society. Since Sallie's death ten years ago I have married Pat Bromley. She plays bowls and recently won the Visitor Cup. Through her, I started playing bowls at sixty-seven and got into the team at Luneside on Fairfield Road. I won the Merit Prize when I was seventy-four. I have roughly three hundred sports trophies altogether. It just shows that it doesn't matter what age you are, if you keep taking the pills and get a good doctor to look after you: even at the age of seventy-six I'm competing quite merrily and hoping to have a few more years. You could say I'm still living the life of Riley!

Ken Riley (b. 1928)

Whippet racing

Robin Hargreaves, my dad, got the licence for whippet racing on Quay Meadow, at the back of the Wagon and Horses on the quay. They used to race whippets on there and a lot used to go and watch. My mum, Mamie Hargreaves used to go along and watch. My dad started it and they raced every week on the Quay Meadow. He used to take bets as well. And they used to come from all over to race whippets, from Barrow and Preston. And then they used to go in the Wagon and Horses pub afterwards. It used to be very popular.

Betty Cummings, *née* Hargreaves (b. 1927)

Going to the dogs – competitors and spectators at the popular whippet races on Quay Meadow.

Seven

Moving Here

Cricket brought me to Lancaster

I was born in Bombay, India in 1933. There were six of us boys and we all played cricket. We were a cricketing family. My father was in his fifties when I was born but he was a very modest man who did not talk much about his career. Earlier this year though my son Ian came across a book on the internet, it's a fascinating book, a complete history of Indian cricket from the days of the British Raj and my father, Palwankar Baloo, is in it. He was known as P. Baloo and he and his three brothers were all cricketers. I didn't know any of this until I read this book. I didn't know that my father had been a famous cricketer because he was such a modest person, he never told us.

In Bombay I played cricket at Khar Gymkhana, our local cricket club. In those days the clubs were all called gymkhanas because of the British. My brother Yeshwant was a captain of the all-India Universities team and it was through him that I came to Lancaster. Yeshwant, who was better known here by his nickname Antoo, played professional cricket for Lancaster in 1954/55. Then he went to Manchester University for postgraduate study and returned to India. He kept in contact with his cricketing friends in Lancaster and they arranged for me to come over.

I arrived in Lancaster in summer 1962, the cricket season. Lancaster is a very historical town and I had heard about the town itself but the first impression I got of Lancaster was the people, you know, they're so genuine, accommodating. The main thing was the cricket though. I was very fortunate to get involved with a club like Lancaster. I still feel that Lancaster Cricket Club is the best in the North West. My first contact was with Norman Ellis. My accommodation and a job had all been arranged through the club: I lived on Coverdale Road and worked at Williamson's.

Above left: Vasant Palwankar (left) and batting partner Ram Rajani at the Khar Gymkhana in Bombay.

Above right: Vasant and Maureen Palwankar on their wedding day in 1976.

Vasant Palwankar receiving a trophy on behalf of the Lancaster CC First XI at Lancaster Cricket Club, Lune Road, 1977.

When I first saw the cricket club it looked so old. It was so darkly lit you could hardly see the team sheet. But we had a good, close-knit team and we used to have a lot of banter and leg-pulling. I got right into it. They were a good set of lads and I had no problems at all settling in. The friends I made were from cricket. In those days, not like now, you had to put your own nets and everything away yourselves. The cricket club was run on a voluntary basis. Also, in India in those days we didn't have pubs and when I came to Lancaster Cricket Club it was so fascinating for me that after the match all the players got together and had a drink, you know. That was a vast difference. I really enjoyed it, after the match we'd all get changed and go in the bar and discuss the game.

When I came here I was fascinated by the chimneys on the houses with smoke coming out of them. Everyone here had coal fires then but we had fires only for cooking in Bombay, we didn't need them for warmth. I am so fascinated by coal fires that even though we have gas I still have a coal fire in the back room of our house for old times' sake. And in my first winter here there was a blizzard; 1962/63 was a severe winter, and I had never seen snow before, it was always sunshine in Bombay.

Altogether, I played for Lancaster for nearly twenty years, one season professionally in 1968. I also played one season for Morecambe and two seasons for Carnforth. In the early 1970s I went to Holland for two years to work as professional cricket coach for a club called Excelsior in Rotterdam. When I came back to Lancaster I married a local girl, Maureen Schofield. We had to get married on a Wednesday afternoon because I played cricket Saturday and Sunday. The weekend that we married I was away playing in a cup match on the Sunday!

I have so many fond memories of Lancaster Cricket Club, like the 1977 season when we were Northern League Division One Champions, winners of the Matthew Brown Trophy and runners-up in the Lancashire Cup. I also made many good friends: one particular gentleman, Mr Dick Chapman, he always used to pull my leg, we used to have a good laugh; Geoff Bates, he was our best man; David Duncan and Mike Speak. One man in particular, Norman Ellis, the present president of Lancaster Cricket Club, I have a very high regard for him because he has made the cricket club what it is now. He's worked for Lancaster Cricket Club for over fifty years and he's a gentleman. To me, he is 'Mr Cricket'.

There must be something good about Lancaster, that's why I stayed. I've never had any problems with racism at all in Lancaster. I like the people very much and I also like the local sense of humour which I find fascinating. You've got to have a laugh. I enjoy mixing with different people; it enriches your perspective on life. I was twenty-eight when I came over here forty-two years ago and my brothers are all back in Bombay. I've been back to Bombay three or four times but it has changed so much since I left that I feel more at home here now after all these years. I was lucky to find a place like Lancaster.

Vasant Palwankar (b. 1933)

A cricketing dynasty

After our interview, intrigued by Vasant's reference to his late father, I decided to further investigate the life of Palwankar Baloo and came upon an incredible story. Through his cricketing prowess, Vasant's father actually became an Indian national hero and role model, a major force in modernising the politics of his country by challenging the prejudices of the Hindu caste system and an inspiration for the great statesman Mahatma Gandhi. In the early twentieth century, cricket teams in India were strictly segregated along both racial and religious lines, for example, British, Parsi, Muslim and Hindu. Furthermore, Hindus were subject to the caste system whereby higher castes would not associate with lower

castes. The Brahmins were the highest caste and the lowest castes of this oppressive system were known as 'Untouchables' because it was widely believed that higher castes would be polluted if they touched them. Against this background, Palwankar Baloo, an Untouchable of the lowly Chamaar caste was invited into a Brahmin cricket team, such was his skill as a slow bowler. He went on to lead the Hindus against European teams and tour England with the first all-India side in 1911, where he took more than 100 wickets. Incredibly, his three brothers also became leading cricketers and in 1923, in an unprecedented move, his brother Vithal was carried on the shoulders of high-caste teammates after captaining the Hindu side in a victorious tournament. In his book *A Corner of a Foreign Field: The Indian History of a British Sport*, Ramachandra Guha hails Baloo as 'the first great Indian cricketer and a pioneer in the emancipation of the Untouchables.'

Sharon Lambert

We built a Polish community in Lancaster

I was born in Lomza, Poland in 1930. The war came and then my father, an army officer, was transferred to north-east Poland to a place called Osowiecz, Grajewo. We lived there but then my father was sent to the front to fight. We lost our home on the 1 September 1939 and we never went back there ever again. From thereon during the war we had to move from one auntie to another until 1941 when the Germans attacked Russia and pushed them back out of this part of Poland. We moved back to my grandmother's in Lomza. Unfortunately, her pottery business was taken over, first of all by the Soviets and then the Germans. The Soviets threw my grandmother out of the house; the Germans gave her the house back but kept the business. We found a roof over our heads there after travelling from

Dancers, including Hanna and Marian Przewozniak, in the Polish Centre, Lancaster.

place to place from '39 till '41. We were there till 1944.

My father was away fighting at the front and my mother was not registered because, being an officer's wife, she'd be sent to a concentration camp. My sister was hiding away as well because at that time she was fourteen or fifteen and she would be taken to the forced labour camp in Germany. So for most of the time she slept in the cellar or in barns, places like that.

In 1944 there was an offensive from the Soviet Union pushing the Germans back to Berlin and my grandmother's house was burnt with artillery shells. So yet again we became homeless. My mother had some friends in Warsaw and for the first time, after four years of no school, I went to school and I had to catch up. I passed all my grammar school exams despite not going to school for four years.

Warsaw was torn down by war and ninety per cent of buildings were destroyed. We lived only in one room, in a building where there was just that room not destroyed. Coming home from school each day, I was opening the door and there was no roof just a staircase, and the sun was either shining or it was raining. We were like swallows in a nest. It was an experience in life of how people can survive.

After the war it became so-called independent Poland but it was like a satellite to the Soviet Union and because my father was a prisoner of war in the Soviet Union we were in a very dangerous situation. He had joined the army of General Anders, who was under British Army command, and they got out of the Soviet Union, due to an agreement with the Allies, into Iran, Iraq, Syria, Jordan, Palestine, Egypt and Italy. After the war ended the whole Polish army was transferred in 1946 to England. And then they got a choice: they could either go back to Poland, or they were granted political asylum in Great Britain, or they were given the option to go to Canada, the United States or Australia. My father decided to stay in Great Britain but we were endangered because he did not come back to Poland. If he came back, he'd be sent to Siberia or another prison camp and exactly the same fate was awaiting us.

My father arrived in this country in 1946 with the army from Italy but we had to be smuggled out from Poland because my father was in England and we would be called British spies or something similar to that and they would take us and either shoot us or send us to prison or away to Siberia. There was an organisation in Great Britain which was bringing people over through the border, they had their own guides. We came with the British Army in transit through East Germany and into West Germany. The Soviets were not allowed to look inside the military vehicles of the British Army. We stayed in West Germany from April until 1 August because they had to check everything. This was 1947.

On 1 August 1947, we arrived at Tilbury in London and my father met us there and brought us to the camp at Flookburgh, where he was in charge of the Polish Resettlement Corps. He thought my sister and I should finish our education in Polish, so he sent us to boarding school. We stayed in a beautiful castle in Perthshire at first and in Spring 1948 the school was transferred to Grendon Hall, near Aylesbury in Buckinghamshire. The whole school was Polish.

After finishing school, I came back north and when my father finished in the Polish Resettlement Corps, he got a house on Myndon Street in Lancaster so we stayed here. A lot of Poles went to London because there were better job opportunities but my father was so tired of war and he found Lancaster very peaceful, very tranquil. He used to love to take a trip to the countryside every Sunday in a bus.

My sister and I both married Polish men because at that time we were not mixing very much with English people. The men had more English wives because there were a lot of Polish men but very few Polish girls. There were 150,000 Polish Army men in England so there were a lot of mixed marriages but they were mostly Polish men and English ladies, particularly in Blackpool where there were a lot of Polish airmen, they nearly all had English wives. I married Marian, who had also come here with the Polish Army, in 1952.

Since we arrived in Lancaster in 1949 I have been very involved with the Polish community. My father brought the first Polish priest here and organised the community. In the beginning there were only young single men but we started the first Polish school when the children arrived in the 1950s. To begin with it was quite a small school but then it started to grow until we had at least 100 children learning the Polish language. We also had Polish dancers, Scouts and Guides. At first we leased a building next to the cathedral but it was pulled down to build the Cathedral Social Centre. So we moved over to a house near Lancaster Castle and we stayed there until 1984 when we bought this building in Nelson Street. It was an old church and hall which we renovated with our own hands and pockets.

It is very important to keep the Polish culture and language because otherwise there would be no community today, although they are coming again now since Poland joined the EC. It was almost like a little self-sufficient community that we had to bring up in the Polish spirit because we had to show the world that nobody could go back to Poland because Poland was not free. We still have a Polish priest and we keep the priest, his car, the church and the church hall. Everything is paid for by our members through organising membership fees, dinner dances, lotteries and renting out the hall. We started in 1950 and fifty-odd years on we're still here.

Hanna Przewozniak, *née* Bargielska (b. 1930)

An Irish nurse in wartime England

I was born in Kilmovee, County Mayo in 1917. I was one of twelve children: seven boys

1st Lieutenant Bridie Duffy, Hamburg, 1947.

and five girls. We had a lovely happy child-hood on the farm and plenty of fresh food. I came over to England in 1939 to do nursing. My sister had come over to do nursing before me and I thought 'that's what I want to do'. Nobody thought I'd stick it but I loved every day of it, to be able to help people who were suffering. I trained as an SRN at Lewisham Hospital in London and then I did a part one midwifery course because you needed that to get a sister's post. The war was raging while I was training and bombs were dropping on London every night. Casualties were coming and going in the hospital all the time. Our church was hit once but the lovely big statue of Christ outside it wasn't touched. TB was also rife and I knew some nurses who went down with it.

In 1944 I joined Queen Alexandra's Imperial Nursing Service and was posted to Hatfield House and then to the 73rd British General Hospital in Normandy. We didn't know where we were going to, it was very hush-hush. My people didn't know where I was. There were thousands of troops there at Southampton when we were going on the ship. Anyway, by the light of the morning we saw that we were going to arrive on the beaches of Arramanches and we waded ashore knee-deep in water and then we were bundled into trucks. That was in July 1944 and the general pointed out to us the severe fighting that was going on in Caen. You could see the smokescreen rising. Oh it was hectic; the wounded were coming in all the time. The great thing was, we were able to evacuate them the next day, over to England, and that kept them in great form. Some of them had terrible wounds and they were only boys, all of them. It was terrible.

It wasn't all sadness though. One time, there was this lad sitting up in bed and he said: 'Haven't you got a brother Tommy Duffy?' And he was from home, from Carracastle in Mayo. He was lucky, he only got a slight wound on the arm. There was a great social life in Normandy too. We were at some American parties. Oh my God! There was this night we went to a party where they had this bowl of cocktail drink and it was beautiful. And after one drink I was just going to have another cup and suddenly this sister dropped down on the floor beside me. She'd been drinking it all night. And I put my cup back!

We were there from July until September when we were posted back to England because the fighting had moved up and they were sending the English hospitals up to Brussels. We were sent back to Chichester House in Sussex, a big posh house, and then we were posted to India, to a convent in Calcutta that had been converted to a hospital. They were all Indian troops that we were treating and we didn't speak Urdu and they didn't speak English but we managed. Poliomyelitis was widespread in Calcutta then. We were also supposed to take these tablets to prevent malaria but we were all going as yellow as a duck's foot with them and we stopped taking them. But the matron said: 'Take your whisky ration.' And I swear that whisky ration saved us. You used to get a bottle of whisky between four of you and you drank so much of this every day, a ration. I never got fond of it but I took it. It killed the germs I'm sure.

We were in India until the Japanese surrendered and the week after that we were posted to Singapore. We had to have eight minesweepers to take us into Singapore. A lot of ships were lost in that area. There, we took in all the prisoners of war, you know, from that awful Changi prison. They were in a terrible state. From Singapore they were going to post me to Bangkok, where there was an outbreak of poliomyelitis, but I got laryngitis and I was sent back to Chichester in England. Then we were posted straight to Germany and I was there a few months before I was demobbed in 1947. I got three medals for my service in the QA's: the France and Germany Star, the Defence Medal and the War Medal 1939-45.

After I was demobbed I worked as a sister in Dartford in Kent. Then my father became ill and I went home to Ireland to nurse him and my mother wasn't so good then and I nursed her. When I came back to England I worked at Preston Royal and then I applied to Lancaster to work as a ward sister at Longlands Annexe. They used to bring patients there from the RLI after their operations.

I married my late husband Robert, who was from Northern Ireland, in Lancaster in 1954 and we had three children, Marie, Angela and Robert. I thought Lancaster was lovely when I first came here over fifty years ago and I still think it's lovely. When the children were young we used to love to go down to Heysham. We went to Morecambe a lot as well and we used to go swimming when they had the big swimming pool there. And

I never made chips, so always when we went out we'd have fish and chips as a treat. I also used to enjoy going with my husband to the Catholic Club, which was over the Alexandra Hotel, and dancing to Irish music. I love living in Lancaster. My son Robert used to say to me: 'Wouldn't it be lovely if you could come down to live in Worthing?' No. I've been here fifty years now and I wouldn't live anywhere else but Lancaster.

Bridie McLaughlin, *née* Duffy (b. 1917)

From Genoa to the Lancashire music halls

My mum's name was Ginocchio before she was married. My mam married Robin Hargreaves. Stephen Ginocchio, the original one, that was my mother's grandfather, in 18-something he

Stephen Ginocchio, a music hall artiste originally from Genoa, Italy, settled in Lancaster in the late nineteenth century.

A mainly Irish group photo outside the John O'Gaunt Hotel on Market Street (*c.*1961), including, kneeling front row: Michael McCann, Jimmy Rodgers, Bert Devane. Standing second row: Chris McGuiness, Billy Murtagh, -?-, Barney Deehan.

came over from Italy, Genoa. I think that the photo I have of him was in his stage clothes. He used to whistle, bird whistle, on stage. He could imitate any bird going, my mum said, and you could hear him even without a microphone. He worked the music halls. My mum used to say when he first came from Italy he used to interpret for the police station, for these boats coming up the Lune. He used to speak a few languages, not just Italian. He came from Italy and there was three sons Jacob, Anthony (my grandad) and Dominic, and two girls, Angelina and Sarah and they were born in Atherton. He lost his first wife and then he married somebody called Jane Schofield… He was on the music halls and he worked his way up to Preston and ended up living in Lancaster. And then he was a labourer after that and made ice-cream. He used to go supping with the Macari's.

Joan Herman, *née* Hargreaves

My nickname was Paddy

Three of my grandparents were Irish. They came over here when the famine was on. She was born in Barrow-in-Furness was my mother. Me dad's mother was called Gallagher and me mother's mother was called Connolly and she married a guy called Traynor. The Adams grandfather came from the Midlands actually – that was the only one that spoilt it! I went to St Peter's school when I was five years of age. Of course me and me brother were always called Paddy Adams, that was me nickname as a child, I never got called Charlie at school.

Charlie Adams (b. 1917)